Untold stories
of a Breadwinner

"A MEMOIR OF SURVIVAL, SACRIFICE, AND BECOMING"

Written by:
Zandra Mae Cochrane

Untold stories of a Breadwinner

Written by Zandra Mae Cochrane
ISBN: 978-1-7644630-4-1

All rights reserved.
No part of this book may be reproduced, stored in a retrieval system,
or transmitted in any form or by any means—electronic, mechanical, photocopying, recording, or otherwise—without prior written permission of the publisher.

Printed in Australia

First edition, 2025

To my children — Hanie, Zach and Jack.
You are the reason I kept going when life tried to break me.
Every sacrifice, every tear, every chapter of this story was written with you in my heart.
You are my strength, my purpose, and my greatest victory.

To every breadwinner who carries the weight of a family in silence.
This book is for you.
For your unseen sacrifices.
For your quiet courage.
For the dreams you keep alive even when you are tired.

May you find comfort in knowing you are not alone.

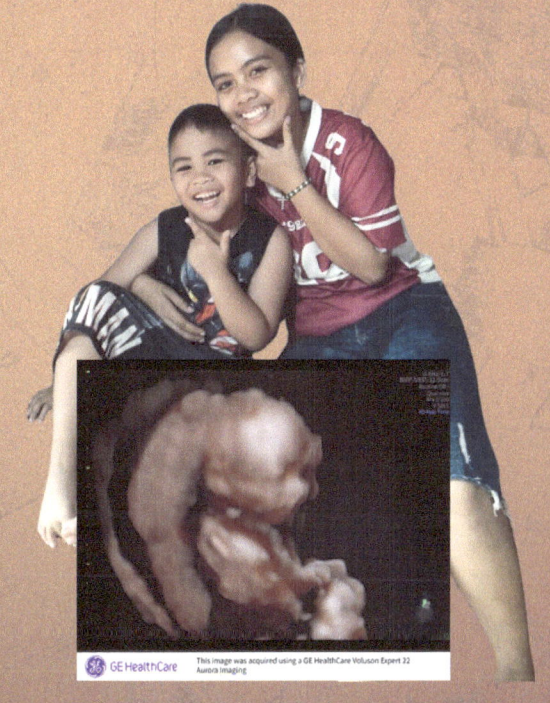

ACKNOWLEDGMENT

To my mother, Miramar —
Our journey was not easy, but it shaped me into the woman I am today.
Thank you for the strength you passed on to me, even in the moments we didn't understand each other.

To my father, Jimmy —
Your life, your struggles, and your love — in all its imperfect forms — taught me resilience.
Your story lives in every page of this book.

To my brother, James —
Thank you for being part of the life I fought so hard to support.

To my friends, mentors, and the people who believed in me —
Your kindness carried me through moments when I felt invisible.
Your encouragement reminded me that my story mattered.

To every person who helped me, even in small ways —
A loan, a word of advice, a moment of understanding —
You became part of my survival.

And finally, to myself —
For choosing to rise.
For choosing to heal.
For choosing to tell this story.

About the author

Zandra Mae "Zandy" — Filipina migrant, mother of two, and resilient heart behind The Untold Stories of a Breadwinner.

Born and raised in the Philippines, Zandra grew up navigating poverty, responsibility, and the expectations placed on her as the eldest daughter. She became a mother at a young age, a teacher in a remote community, a provider for her entire family, and eventually an OFW who rebuilt her life in Australia.

Her writing is shaped by lived experience — the quiet sacrifices, the unseen battles, and the emotional strength required to carry a family through hardship.

Today, she continues to build a new life abroad while raising her children, creating educational resources, and sharing her story to empower women, migrants, and breadwinners around the world.

The Untold Stories of a Breadwinner is her first memoir — a testament to courage, survival, and the power of choosing yourself.

FOREWORD

There are stories people see, and there are stories people never ask about. This book is about the second kind.

For most of my life, I carried responsibilities that were too heavy for my age, my heart, and my circumstances. I became a mother early, a provider early, and a survivor long before I understood what survival really meant. I worked jobs I never planned for, endured judgment I didn't deserve, and held together a family that often didn't see the weight I carried.

But this is not a story of bitterness. It is a story of becoming. I wrote this memoir because breadwinners rarely get to speak. We are expected to endure quietly, to sacrifice without question, to give without rest.

Our stories are often hidden behind the success of others. This book is my truth — the parts of my life that were never spoken, never acknowledged, never understood. It is for every woman who has ever felt alone in her struggles, every migrant who has ever started over, every mother who has ever carried more than she could hold.

If you are reading this, I hope you find strength in my journey. I hope you see your own courage reflected in these pages. And I hope you remember that even the quietest stories deserve to be told.

Memories we never forget....

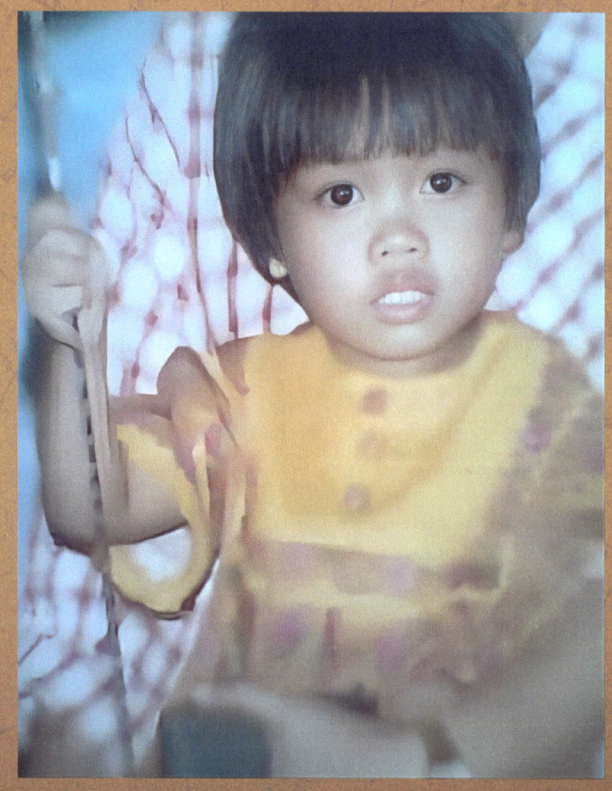

CHAPTER 1
THE CITY THAT RAISED ME

Before the province, before the fresh air and quiet nights, there was the city — loud, crowded, and alive in a way that shaped the earliest version of me. Our house there was simple, made mostly of wood, with a roof that had more holes than we could count. When it rained, we placed basins everywhere, catching the water that dripped through like tiny reminders of the life we were living.

We had one bedroom, and that was where all of us slept, bodies lined up beside each other, sharing the same floor. YES, no bed, no electric fans or mattress, just a taditional handwooven mat we called it "Banig", pillow, mosquito net and blanket is enought. The living room was small, the kind of space where one piece of furniture already felt like too much. And the kitchen — that was something else entirely. We didn't have a gas stove like people have now. We had a pabilo — a rolled cloth dipped into a bottle of kerosene, lit carefully, the flame dancing dangerously close to the wooden walls. That was how we cooked our meals.

My mother ran a tiny sari-sari store in front of our house. It wasn't much, but it kept us going. Behind the store was our bathroom, which also doubled as the pigpen. In the Philippines, that wasn't unusual. Many families raised pigs beside their homes, feeding them scraps, hoping to sell them later for a bit of money. The smell was strong, the noise constant, but that was our life.

Our neighbourhood was loud — the kind of loud that never really stops. Lechoneros roasted pigs early in the morning, gamblers argued over bets, and people shouted across houses as if distance didn't exist. But behind our house lived someone who brought warmth into all that chaos: Nanay Pani. She was my parents' closest friend, and she always said she helped take care of me when I was little. She loved telling the story of how I would dance whenever someone said "sayaw," no hesitation, no shyness — just joy.

Beside our house ran a small canal, and beside that canal stood a tall Talisay tree. That was our playground. My friends and I didn't care if the water was dirty or if the soil had worms. We played with whatever we found — mud, leaves, stones — and we were happy. Childhood didn't ask for much.

Every morning and afternoon, I had a job: collecting "lamaw" — food scraps from different houses — to feed our pig. I walked from house to house with a bucket, knocking on doors, asking for leftovers. Sometimes I even went as far as the department store near us. I knew the back entrance that led to the kitchen. When the chef was drunk or slow, I would sneak in, carrying my little brother on my back. I didn't care if my shirt was dirty or if I smelled like the pigpen. I just wanted to take him to the toy section, even if we couldn't buy anything.

One day, I got into trouble. My brother saw a toy he liked — a small yoyo with lights — and he screamed because he wanted it. I had no money. I panicked. I grabbed him, ran back to the kitchen, and yelled at him to help me get the food scraps. The bucket was heavy — heavier than I expected — and I struggled to carry it home. My uncles and aunties used to joke that maybe that's why I didn't grow tall, because I carried too many heavy things as a child.

After collecting lamaw, I had another task: gathering kangkong leaves from the pond to feed the pig. My mother still bought feeds, but this was part of the routine. I never complained. Kids back then didn't complain. You just did what you were told. Not because you were brave, but because you didn't know any other way.By the time I reached elementary school, I was already helping my mother sell the delicacies she cooked. She molded them using the lids of empty Nescafé bottles, placing banana leaves on top. Everything had to be sold. Nothing could go to waste.

I studied, I played when I could, but people mostly saw me as the child who could read and write — something rare on my father's side of the family. None of them knew how to read. My father didn't either. But when it came to money, to numbers, to computation — especially gambling math — he was a genius. You couldn't trick him. He could calculate bets faster than anyone I knew.

That was my life in the city — noisy, messy, poor, but full of moments that shaped the strength I didn't know I was building. I didn't realise it then, but every bucket of lamaw, every morning chore, every heavy load I carried was preparing me for the life ahead — the life of a breadwinner.

Growing up, we were always taught to be content

with whatever we had. No demands, no asking for more — because there was nothing more to ask for. Life on that crowded street started early. By five in the morning, people were already outside their houses: sweeping leaves, feeding their animals, sipping coffee while reading old newspapers, or checking their lottery numbers with quiet hope. And because the houses stood so close together, every sound travelled — the laughter, the gossip, the clatter of pots, even the arguments of husbands and wives from the other side of the wall. We heard everything. We were not exempted from that noise.

There were nights when my parents fought too, throwing things, shouting words I didn't understand. I would cry silently while holding my brother, trying to keep him calm.Some nights were worse. I remember being woken up at eleven or twelve midnight, still half-asleep, carrying my brother as my mother dragged us along the dark streets, following my father wherever he had gone. We walked for kilometres, but I didn't mind. I was only eight or nine, too young to understand what was happening, too young to feel anger, too young to feel fear. All I cared about were the dreams in my head — dreams that I was like in another world.

As I grew older, my emotions began to take shape. I started excelling in school. Even though life was hard and money was always tight, my parents somehow managed to send me to a private Catholic school run by nuns. The only requirement was my grades and reading ability in English — as long as I stayed at the top, I could stay in the school. And I did. Every year.

Medals and ribbons should have made any child feel proud, but in our house, they were simply reminders that I had to finish quickly, because responsibilities were waiting. My mother always reminded me that once my brother started school, I had to help carry the load.

 He didn't get into the same school I did, but that wasn't the issue. What hurt more was the feeling that he was the favourite. I started to get jealous, quietly, secretly. It felt like no matter how hard I worked, no matter how many medals
I brought home, there was always a child who was loved a little more. That was my thoughts before.

 My classmates lived a life so different from mine. It was a big private school in the city — most of them arrived in cars,
with nannies carrying their bags. They had roller backpacks, matching lunchboxes, pencil cases that sparkled, and shoes that never looked worn. Sometimes I wished I had those things too. But I learned early not to mind what others had. I was contented with what I was given — clothes and shoes from "ukay-ukay" or secondhand things sold in the market, hand-me-down bags. That was my life. And somehow, even then, I carried it with quiet pride. All I care is, I have something that I can use for school. No toys but books. The doll that was given to me then were kept inside the cabinet. We were not allowed to play for it. My mother used to believed that whatever gifts you receive, kept it and ntake care of it. Playing wasn't included at all even if you cry but of course you can touch and

imagined how beautiful it is in your eyes.

And every day, rain or shine, starting year one up to year six, I walked five kilometers to school and five kilometers back home. That was the life. I walked with my neighbours who were the same age as me — their school was just next to mine. We didn't complain. We didn't compare. We just walked, laughing, talking, playing along the way. All you could hear from us were the sounds of joy, the kind only children can make even in the middle of hardship.

That was the city I used to live in — noisy, messy, difficult, but full of moments that shaped the strength I didn't know I was building.

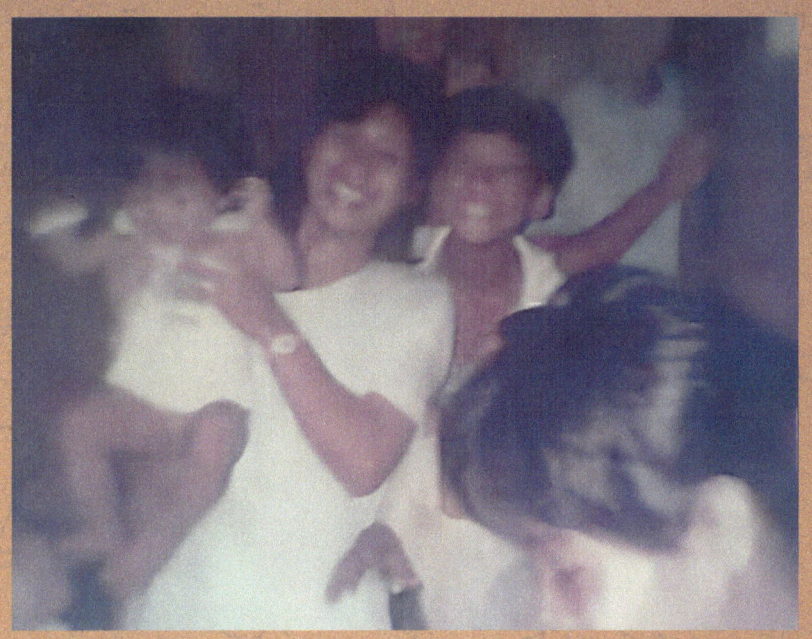

CHAPTER 2
THE BET TAKER

My father lived in a world of noise — a world of feathers, fists, and fast money. He was a "kristo", a bet taker in the cockfighting arena or "sabungan" in our language, it was like a second home to him. If the city was loud, the sabungan was louder. Men shouting numbers, roosters crowing, coins clinking, curses flying through the air like arrows. That was the soundtrack of his life.

He didn't finish school. He barely made it past elementary. But when it came to money — especially gambling money — he was sharper than anyone I knew. You couldn't trick him. He could calculate bets faster than a calculator, faster than the men who tried to cheat him. Numbers were his language, even if letters weren't.

But the sabungan didn't give stability. It gave hope one day and disappointment the next. Some days he came home with pockets full of cash, smiling, generous, ready to buy food for the house. Other days he came home empty-handed, quiet, avoiding my mother's eyes. I learned early that the sound of his footsteps outside the door could tell us what kind of night we were about to have. Sometimes it's scary.

My father wasn't a bad man. He wasn't a dreamer either. He lived day by day, bet by bet, peso by peso. Maybe it was because no one taught him to want more. Maybe it was because life never gave him the chance to imagine anything beyond survival. I didn't understand that as a child. I only saw the man who left early, came home late, and carried the weight of a life he didn't know how to change.

Still, there were moments when he felt like a hero to us. I remember how, whenever he arrived home — whether in the middle of the night or early morning — he would wake us up just to show what he brought. Bread. SkyFlakes. KingFlakes in a tin can. That is tge most popular biscuits before. Sometimes even a big Rebisco can, the kind that felt like treasure to children like us. We would sit up, sleepy-eyed but excited, eating biscuits as if they were gifts from another world. Those were the moments that made us happy.

But there was another side to him too. When he got angry, he could scare you with just his eyes — sharp, intense, like he could kill you with a stare. But he never laid a hand on us. Not once. His anger lived in his face, not in his fists.

And he wasn't always hard. He used to take us to free cottage beaches, the kind where you didn't have to pay for anything except the food you brought. He took us to church every Sunday, sitting beside us as if that routine was his way of keeping our family together. But one day, he just stopped. The routines disappeared. The Sundays changed. He became different. That's when I knew something was wrong. I saw my mother cry, but I never asked why. I just knew something was off. He stopped celebrating birthdays with us too — not that birthdays were grand in our family. Lighting a candle in church and eating native chicken with rice was already a feast. But even that small tradition faded.

Some nights were worse than others. There were times when my mother woke us up at midnight, telling us to get up, telling us we had to go. I would carry my brother, still half-asleep, as we followed her through the dark streets, searching for my father. We walked for kilometres, but I didn't complain. I was only eight or nine.

I didn't understand what was happening. I didn't know why they fought, why we had to chase him, why our nights were filled with fear instead of rest. All I had were the dreams in my mind — dreams I was so happy in another world, like any other child had.

Despite everything, I loved my father. Children love without conditions, without explanations. I loved him when he came home with money. I loved him when he came home with nothing. I loved him when he was loud, when he was quiet, when he was lost in his own world. I loved him even when I didn't understand him.

And maybe that's why I grew up fast. Maybe that's why I learned to carry things — responsibilities, emotions, expectations — long before I should have. My father teach me how to dream and taught me how to endure every pain. He taught me how to read people, how to sense danger, how to stay alert. He taught me that life doesn't always give you choices, but you still have to keep going.

Looking back now, I realise something I couldn't see

then:
My father wasn't just a bet taker or a gambler.
He was a man trying to survive the only way he knew how. Back the, I never understand as a kid who carried lots of emotions.
And in his own imperfect way, I thanked him because he shaped the breadwinner I would one day become.

CHAPTER 3
THE DREAMER WHO LOST HER DREAMS

My mother was a woman of quiet strength — the kind of strength that doesn't shout, doesn't demand, doesn't break things when life gets heavy. She carried her disappointments differently. They lived in her eyes, in the way she sighed after a long day, in the way she stared out the old wooden window as if remembering a life she once imagined for herself.

Before she married my father, she had her own small businesses. She was independent, resourceful, and determined. People said she was smart and rich, that she could have built something bigger if life had given her the chance. But marriage, children, and the weight of survival changed her path. Slowly, her dreams shrank into the size of our small wooden house, into the corners of our sari-sari store, into the routines she repeated every day.

My mother was not a crowded person. She didn't need people around her to feel whole. She enjoyed her own company, preferred silence over noise, and believed that having fewer friends meant fewer disappointments. She survived on her own strength — a strength that amazed me even as a child. Whatever money she received from my father, whether it was a small amount or a rare bigger one, she made sure it lasted. She budgeted every peso with the precision of someone who had learned to stretch nothing into something.

She used to say she never wanted kids. She said it

openly, especially when me and my brother fought like children do. I remember her saying, half in frustration and half in truth, that it would have been better if she had taken us away when we were little — that she didn't want children, but because she had us, she had no choice but to raise us. Those words stung and painful, even if I didn't fully understand them then. But now, looking back, I know they came from exhaustion, not hatred. From a woman who carried too much and had no one to help her carry it.

Yet she had her soft sides too. She loved travelling, even if she rarely had the chance. She wanted to explore places where she could grow, where she could breathe, where she could be more than a wife, more than a mother, more than a woman trapped by circumstances. That desire to see the world — that restless curiosity — is something I inherited from her. One of the few traits she passed on willingly.

She woke up before the sun, preparing the store, boiling water, arranging the goods on the shelves. She cooked delicacies to sell — molding them in empty Nescafé lids, covering them with banana leaves and that's her "biko", a popular filipino delicacy hoping every piece would be bought so nothing went to waste. She fed the pig, cleaned the house, managed the store, stretched every peso, and still found a way to keep us fed, clothed, and in school.

But behind all that strength was a woman who was tired. A woman who wanted more but didn't know how to reach for it anymore.

I saw it in the way she looked at other families.
I saw it in the way she held her breath when my father came home empty-handed.
I saw it in the way she cried quietly at night, thinking we were asleep.
She never talked about her pain. She never explained her sadness. She just kept going, as if survival was the only dream she was allowed to keep.

There were days when she was soft — brushing my hair, telling me stories, laughing at small things. And there were days when she was sharp, her voice rising with frustration, her patience thin from carrying too much. I didn't understand her then. I only saw the surface: the strictness, the expectations, the pressure she placed on me to excel in school and every talent. Comparing wasn't new to me from her.

But now I know she wasn't just intentionally being hard.She was being hopeful.She was trying to give me the life she never had.

She pushed me to study, to stay at the top of my class, to earn medals and ribbons — not because she wanted to brag, but because she believed education was the only way out. She believed I could break the cycle she was trapped in. She believed I could become someone she never had the chance to be.But her hope came with weight.A weight I carried quietly.A weight I didn't know how to name.

She didn't celebrate my achievements the way other mothers did. When I brought home medals, she didn't clap or hug me. She simply said, "Padayon" which means keep going. Finish school fast. Your brother will start studying soon." To her, my success wasn't a moment to celebrate — it was a responsibility, a reminder that I had to grow up quickly.

And I did.
I became the child who didn't ask for anything.
 The child who didn't complain.
 The child who understood too early that life was hard and money was tight.
 The child who learned to be content with ukay-ukay clothes and shoes or secondhand things.
 The child who knew her mother was doing her best, even when her best didn't look gentle.

My mother wasn't perfect.
 But she was present.
 She was tired, but she tried.
 She was wounded, but she kept going.
And in her own quiet way, she taught me resilience — the kind that doesn't make noise, the kind that doesn't ask for applause, the kind that survives even when dreams fade.
Looking back now, I realise something I couldn't see as a child:

My mother didn't lose her dreams.
 She gave them to me.

CHAPTER 4
THE MOVE TO THE PROVINCE

We packed our clothes inside old travelling bags — the kind with worn-out zippers and faded fabric. One of them was my father's favourite bag, a bag he kept for years even though it looked tired. We didn't bring much, only the things we needed to survive. But to me, it felt like we were packing a whole new life.

I was excited. Truly excited. The thought of seeing my cousins and relatives made my heart race. Every time we visited the province before, we were treated like celebrities — and yes, it was true. In the Philippines, when you come from the city, people imagine you're living a better life. They think you're not poor, not struggling, not carrying the same burdens they do. But the truth was the opposite. We struggled more in the city than most people in the province ever knew.

My father was good at hiding that. Especially when it came to money. He had a way of lifting himself up in front of others, maybe because he had no education, maybe because he wanted to feel respected, or maybe because coming from the city gave him a certain pride. And in the province, he owned land — lots of it. But he never believed in farming. He didn't like plowing fields or riding carabaos. To him, farming was the lowest thing he could ever do. I, on the other hand, loved the idea of it. It felt like adventure. But back then, farmers were looked down on — treated as if they were less because they lacked education. People didn't see how skilled they were, how much strength and knowledge it took to grow food. Many farmers struggled, but many were content too. They lived simply, honestly.

The province felt like a different world. Everything was slower, quieter, more grounded. My grandmother, Nanay Telyang — my father's mother — woke up at four in the morning every day. She boiled water for native coffee, watered her plants, and cooked in a kitchen filled with the smell of burning wood and uling or coal. By the time the sun rose, the chickens were already crowing, and people were walking down the street on their way to the farm. The air was fresh — the kind of fresh that fills your lungs and makes you feel alive.

Life here had its own rhythm.
At 6 p.m., the Angelus played.
At night, we prayed the rosary.
It was stricter, more traditional, more rooted in faith.

My aunties and cousins served in the church, and I was the only one in our family who followed that path. Maybe it was the quietness of the province, maybe it was the routine, maybe it was the peace I found in prayer — but I felt drawn to it.

Dinner was at 6:30 p.m., and by 7:30 or 8 p.m., the whole town was asleep. The nights were dark, the kind of dark you don't see in the city. No cars, no shouting, no chaos — just crickets, the wind, and the occasional bark of a dog.

I met new friends, but they treated me differently. To

them, I came from another world — the city. It was like I had stepped off a different planet. They looked at me with curiosity, sometimes admiration, sometimes distance. But I never showed them that they had to treat me any differently. I didn't want to be the "city girl." I just wanted to belong.

The move to the province wasn't just a change of place.
It was a shift in identity.
A shift in how people saw me.
A shift in how I saw myself.
The city raised me.
But the province began to shape me —
quietly, slowly, deeply.

CHAPTER 5
THE CHILD WHO TRIED TO MAKE EVERYONE Proud

I didn't grow up trying to be the best.I grew up trying to be enough. Enough for my mother, who believed education was the only way out. Enough for my father, who drifted in and out of routines like a tide that never stayed.Enough for a family that needed someone to carry the weight they never asked for but always expected.

From the moment I learned how to read, people around me treated it like a miracle. On my father's side, no one could read or write. They were good people — hardworking, street-smart, survivors — but letters were not their language. Numbers were. Money was. Bets were. So when I picked up a book and understood the words, it felt like I had done something extraordinary.

But extraordinary quickly became expected.

I became the child who always had to do her best.I admit I was pressured early.

People kept telling me how good I was — how I could sing, dance, draw, memorize speeches, perform oratorical pieces, and excel in quiz bees. Every talent I had became another reason to push me harder. And somehow, all those compliments shaped me into someone who felt responsible for making everyone proud, especially on my father's side where education wasn't valued. Finishing elementary was already a struggle for many of them. My father had a sister who became a teacher — the only one — and she became the first example of what I could be. But it was in my generation that education finally became important. When they saw me graduate college — even while pregnant — something shifted. They started to believe it was possible.

But before all of that, I was just a child trying to balance expectations with the little childhood I had. My mother would call me in the middle of my play with friends, asking me to get something she needed from the store. I had to walk kilometers to fetch it, and walk the same distance back. I never complained. I just did it. That was my life — play interrupted by responsibility, childhood interrupted by duty.

Every year, I stood on stage with medals around my neck — gold, silver, ribbons of every colour. My classmates' parents clapped loudly, took photos, hugged their children. My mother didn't clap. She asked someone to get us a picture but sometimes not. She didn't hug me. She simply said, "Padayon" or "keep going". Finish fast. Your brother will start school soon and you need to get a job soon."

To her, my medals weren't accomplishments. Respect and discipline matters her most. They were reminders.Reminders that I had to grow up quickly.Reminders that I had to help carry the family.Reminders that childhood was something I couldn't afford to keep. And so I tried harder.I studied longer.I behaved better.I asked for nothing.

I learned to be content with what was given and in my hands. I learned to smile even when I wanted to cry. I learned to hide my jealousy when my brother received attention I never did. I learned to swallow the ache of wanting to be the favourite child — or at least a favourite child.

I walked many kilometers to school every day, rain or shine, with my neighbours beside me. Their school was next to mine, and we laughed the whole way, our feet muddy, our uniforms damp, our hearts light. Those walks were the only time I felt like a normal child — not a breadwinner in training, not a responsibility carrier, not a future provider. Just a girl with friends, laughing on the road.

But even then, I knew I was different.My classmates came to school in cars, tricycles, with nannies, parents or grandparents carrying their bags. I never experienced that but I never complained. I didn't realized till I came to province that it was a normal thing. Kids walk and go to school by themselves. I thought I was different. They had roller backpacks, matching lunchboxes, pencil cases and notebooks that sparkled. I had a secondhand bag and a quiet determination to prove I belonged there. I didn't envy them. I didn't complain. I simply observed — and worked harder.

I wanted to make everyone proud.

But deep down, I wanted something else too. I wanted someone to be proud of me without needing a reason. I wanted someone to look at me and say, "You did well," not because I carried the family, not because I earned medals, not because I behaved perfectly — but because I was me.
But that kind of love didn't exist in my childhood.

So I created my own version of it.
I became the girl who tried. The girl who endured. The girl who
carried more than she should. The girl who believed that if she worked hard enough, maybe one day, someone would finally see her. Looking back now, I realise something I couldn't understand then:

    I wasn't trying to make everyone proud.
    I was trying to feel worthy of being loved.
And that quiet longing — that silent ache — became the foundation of the breadwinner I would one day become.

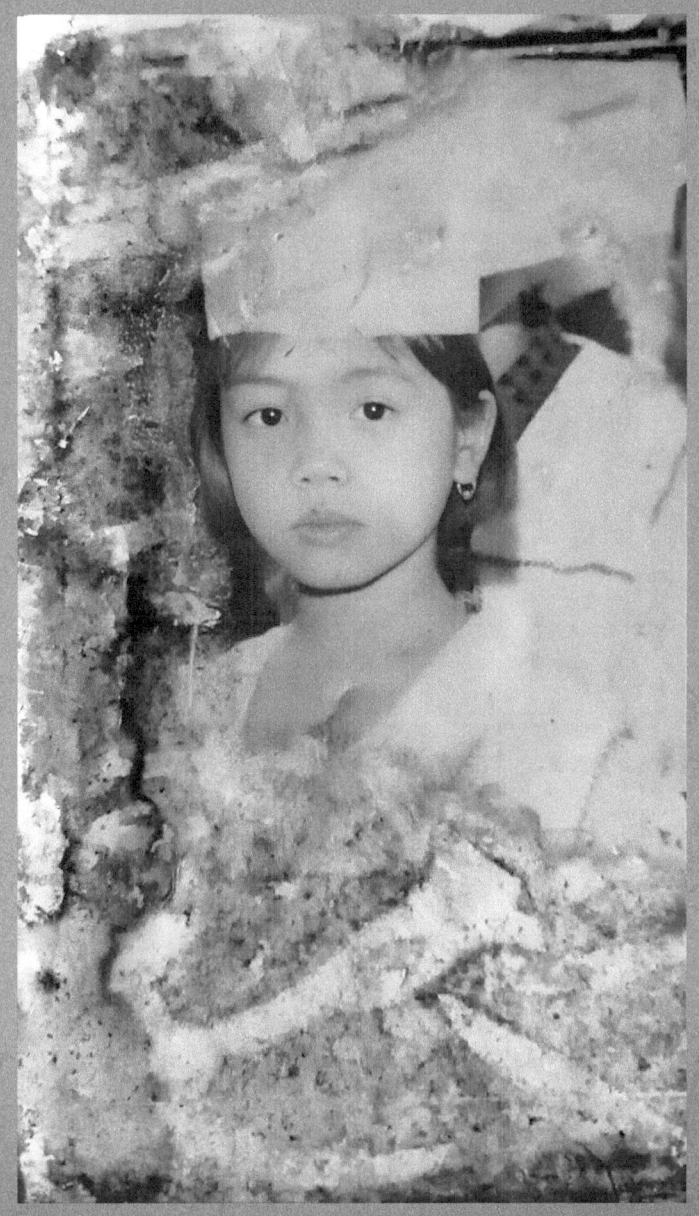

CHAPTER 6
WHEN THE PROVINCE BECAME TOO HEAVY

At first, the province felt like a fresh start — a place where the air was cleaner, the mornings calmer, and the nights quieter. But as the days passed, the silence began to feel heavier. The quietness that once felt peaceful slowly turned into something else — something that made me more aware of the things we didn't talk about, the things we didn't have, the things we were trying to escape.

Life in the province was simple, but simplicity didn't mean ease.It meant work.It meant routine.It meant responsibilities that didn't wait for childhood to finish.Every morning, before the sun even touched the tops of the coconut trees, the whole barangay was already awake. My grandmother boiled water for native coffee, the smell of roasted beans mixing with the smoke from burning wood. Neighbours swept their yards, fed their chickens, prepared for the farm. The sound of footsteps on the dirt road became the province's version of an alarm clock.

And in the middle of all that, I was growing — not just in age, but in awareness. I started to notice the things I didn't see before.The way my mother's face tightened when money was mentioned.The way my father avoided certain conversations.
The way adults whispered when they thought children weren't listening.The province was beautiful, but it was also honest.
It didn't hide struggles the way the city did.It didn't

distract you with noise. It made you face life as it was. And life, for us, was getting heavier. It became too heavy because more responsibilities came — more than I ever expected. I thought I was only dealing with my mother and father, but province life felt like dealing with everyone: family, relatives, neighbours, even friends.

Suddenly, I wasn't just a daughter. I was a helper in my mother's business, a runner for errands, a child expected to show respect to every adult, a girl who had to follow unspoken rules so I wouldn't embarrass the family name. I was only thirteen, but I already felt obligated to everyone. There were things I had to do, and even more things I wasn't allowed to do — not because I didn't want to, but because "rules" said I shouldn't. Gossips were everywhere. One mistake, one wrong move, and it felt like the whole town knew. You'd be doomed before you even understood what you did wrong.

Asking simple questions like "Can I play?" or "Can I visit my friends?" felt impossible. Before I could even think of asking, the house had to be spotless, the yard swept, the dishes washed, the uniforms laundered — and I only had one set of uniform for the whole week. I was already in high school, but childhood still felt like a luxury I wasn't allowed to touch. I had to cook, finish my assignments, and if I was lucky, maybe I could watch a little TV.

I remember one afternoon when my mother sent me to buy something. As I walked past the houses, I saw a neighbour watching Meteor Garden, the most popular novela at that time. I stopped for a few seconds, just to watch through their wooden window. But as soon as they noticed someone outside, they closed it immediately. I hurried home, but my mother was already waiting, angry, yelling that I was selfish. And I remember thinking, No... I wasn't selfish. I just watched TV for a few seconds. But in the province, even seconds felt like sins.

My father owned land here — more than most people knew. But land meant nothing if you didn't believe in farming. And he didn't. He refused to plow fields or ride a carabao. To him, farming was the lowest thing a man could do. To me, it looked like adventure. But to him, it was humiliation. And because he refused to work the land, the land refused to work for us.

So we lived on what my mother could stretch, what my grandmother could grow, and what we could survive on. I helped where I could. Fetching water. Feeding the pigs. Running errands. Doing chores that didn't care if I was tired or still a child. Slowly, something inside me began to shift.

The province, which once felt like a place of freedom, started to feel like a place of expectations. A place where I had to be responsible. A place where I had to be strong. A place where I had to grow up faster than I wanted to. I watched my cousins and neighbours live simpler lives — playing in the fields, swimming in rivers, laughing without worry. They treated me differently because I came from the city, as if I came from another world. But I didn't feel different. I didn't feel special. I felt like a girl trying to find her place in a life that kept changing.

And somewhere between the quiet mornings and the long walks, between the Angelus at six and the rosary at night, between the chores and the expectations, I realised something:
The province wasn't just a place we moved to.
It was a place that demanded a new version of me.
A version who understood silence.
A version who carried responsibility.
A version who learned to hide her fears.
A version who knew that childhood was slipping away.

The city raised me.
But the province —
the province began to shape the woman I would become.

CHAPTER 7
REALISING I WAS GROWING UP TOO FAST

There comes a moment in every child's life when innocence quietly slips away. For some, it happens slowly. For me, it happened all at once — not because I wanted it to, but because life demanded it.

I was only thirteen when I realised I was no longer just a child.Not in the province.Not in my family.Not in the life I was living.

Responsibilities came like waves — one after another, never stopping, never asking if I was ready. At first, I thought I was only dealing with my mother and father. But province life had its own rules, its own expectations, its own invisible weight.

Suddenly, I wasn't just responsible to my parents. I was responsible to everyone.
Family. Relatives.Neighbours.riends.Even people I barely knew.Everyone had something to say. Everyone had something to expect. Everyone had a rule I had to follow.

There were duties in my mother's business, duties in the house, duties in the community. I felt obligated to help, obligated to behave, obligated to be the "good girl" who never made mistakes. And if I did make one — even a small one — it felt like the whole town knew. Gossips travelled faster than the wind. One wrong move and you were doomed, judged, whispered about, watched.

There were things I had to do. And even more things I wasn't allowed to do. Not because I didn't want to. But because "rules" said I shouldn't. Rules created by people. Rules created by fear of embarrassment. Rules created to protect the family name.

Asking simple things like **"Can I play?"** or **"Can I visit my friends?"** felt like asking for the moon. Before I could even think of asking, the house had to be spotless. The yard swept. The dishes washed. The uniforms laundered — and I only had one set of uniform for the entire week. I was already in high school, but childhood still felt like something I had to earn.

I had to cook. I had to study. I had to finish everything before I could even breathe. And if I was lucky, maybe — just maybe — I could watch a little TV.

I remember one afternoon so clearly. My mother sent me to buy something, and as I walked past the houses, I saw a neighbour watching Meteor Garden, the most popular novela at that time. I stopped for a few seconds, just to watch through their wooden window. Just a few seconds. But as soon as they noticed someone outside, they closed the window immediately.

I hurried home, but my mother was already waiting. Angry. Disappointed. She yelled that I was selfish. And I remember thinking, No... I wasn't selfish. I was just watching TV for a few seconds. But in the province, even seconds felt like sins.

That was the moment I realised something painful:I wasn't allowed to be a child anymore.

While other kids played in the fields, swam in rivers, playing kites and laughed without worry, I was learning how to carry responsibilities that didn't belong to me. I was learning how to behave like an adult long before I understood what adulthood meant. Even when I was a child, the way I write my name and paragraph in my notebook are being monitored making it sure it is nice, neat and clean. The way I speak, sit down or even make movements are carefully watched. We are not allowed to speak between the adults conversation when their is family gathering, and if we are caught doing that, you wait for the punishment later. It's either you kneel with salts, let you participate in the novena the whole month, or beat you using the guava stem or bamboo shoots. It was harsh for me that time.

I watched my cousins live simple, carefree lives. They treated me differently because I came from the city — as if I came from another world. But I didn't feel different. I didn't feel special. I felt like a girl trying to survive expectations that kept growing bigger than me.

And somewhere between the chores, the rules, the gossip, and the long walks, I realised:I was growing up too fast.Faster than I wanted.Faster than I understood.Faster than anyone noticed. The province didn't just shape me.It aged me.It pushed me.It forced me to become someone stronger, quieter, more aware.

The province didn't just age me through

responsibilities — it taught me a kind of awareness I never asked for. Here, boys stayed with boys and girls stayed with girls. Even as children, we were expected to follow that invisible line. If you were caught playing with boys, people would start talking — not about you, but about your family, about how you were raised, about what kind of girl you would become. I never understood that. I remember one friend who was simply playing with a boy, and a few weeks later, both families agreed they should "be together" before the town could gossip about them. They were just kids, learning how to communicate, but the adults turned it into something else. It felt cruel for me.

My mother reminded me constantly about these things — the rules, the dangers, the expectations. "If you want to study," she would say, "focus on it. Don't entertain people. Don't give anyone a reason to talk." And so I didn't. It grew me up so fast, faster than I could process. I had to be mature, cautious, aware of every move I made

It's funny now, but back then it terrified me: one of my aunties told us that if we talked to a boy and he held our hand, we would get pregnant. We were all scared. Good thing I was in the special class — the top class — and learned the truth in science. But I kept quiet. Arguing with elders was disrespectful and could bring dishonor to your family. In the province, every mistake a child made was blamed on the parents. Everything had to be accurate, proper, acceptable.

My only escape with the family traditions and beliefs

was reading. At night, using the dim light of a "lampara". It is a small kerosene lamp made of glass and metal, common in Filipino homes before electricity became stable. It has a clear glass chimney that protects the flame, and inside is a cotton wick that soaks up kerosene from the base. When lit, the flame glows softly — warm, steady, and gentle — casting a yellow light that flickers with every movement of the air.

It isn't bright like a bulb. It doesn't light up a whole room.

But it gives just enough light to read, to write, to think, to dream. It has a smell too — a mix of kerosene and warmth — a scent that becomes part of childhood memories. It hums quietly, almost like it's breathing with you. And when the night is dark and the world is quiet, the lampara feels like a companion, a tiny fire that keeps you company.

For many children in the province, including me, the lampara was more than a lamp. It was a doorway —to books, to imagination, to a world bigger than the one outside your window. I read and read and read — books and lampara became my world, my comfort, my freedom. And whenever I watched TV and saw teenagers my age living comfortable lives, laughing, enjoying their youth, I would ask myself quietly, **What would it feel like to experience life that way?**

And from that question, something inside me began to grow. I started dreaming — really dreaming — and fantasizing about a life that felt comfortable, gentle, and free. That's where my aspirations in life began. I told myself that if I kept studying, if I stayed focused, maybe one day I could work, leave the province, and try living the kind of life I only saw on TV. I wondered how it felt to ride a plane. How it felt to eat and order food in restaurants or in Jollibee. How it felt to visit malls and shop for things you actually wanted, not just needed. I imagined myself wearing nice clothes, dresses, even makeup — wondering how I would look, how it would feel to choose something just for me.

All those dreams lived quietly in my head, keeping me company in a world that expected me to grow up too fast.

CHAPTER 8
THE FIRST SIGNS OF BECOMING THE BREADWINNER

I didn't wake up one day and suddenly become the breadwinner.It didn't happen with a big moment or a dramatic announcement.It happened quietly — slowly — in the small, ordinary days of my life in the province.

It began with the little things.
The errands.
The chores.
The expectations.

The unspoken rules that told me I had to be responsible, even when I was still a child.

At thirteen, I already felt the weight of being "the eldest," even though no one said it out loud. I was the one people called when something needed to be done. I was the one my mother relied on when she needed help in the store. I was the one relatives asked favours from because "Si Zandra, maayo man na siya" or it means "Zandy, is so good at any work". I was the one neighbours trusted to run errands because they knew I wouldn't complain.

And I didn't.I just did what was asked.Because that was the life I knew.But somewhere in those routines, I started to notice a shift — not in the world, but in myself. I was becoming the person who solved things.

The person who carried things. The person who made things easier for others.The first signs of becoming the breadwinner weren't heroic.They were subtle.They were quiet.They were woven into the everyday moments of my childhood.

I learned to read people's moods.I learned to sense tension before it exploded.I learned to adjust myself depending on who was around. learned to be careful with my words, my actions, my presence.I learned to survive.

My mother depended on me more than she admitted. She would call me in the middle of my play, asking me to buy something from the store miles away. I would walk the long road, dust clinging to my legs, the sun burning my skin, and walk the same distance back. I didn't question it. I didn't ask why it had to be me. I just went.

My father depended on me too, in his own way. He didn't say it, but I could feel it — the pride he had when I excelled in school, the way he introduced me to relatives, the way he looked at me when I read something out loud. I was his proof that life could be different. That someone in the family could rise above the struggles he never escaped.

And the province, with all its rules and expectations, shaped me even more.I had to be careful.I had to be proper. I had to be the girl who didn't give anyone a reason to talk.Because in the province, one mistake wasn't just your mistake — it became your family's shame.

So I learned to carry myself with caution.I learned to protect my family's name.I learned to be the "good girl," even when I didn't understand why it mattered so much.But inside, something else was growing — something stronger than fear, stronger than pressure, stronger than the rules that tried to shape me.

Dreams. The dreams that started in the glow of a lampara.The dreams that whispered to me while I read books at night.The dreams that grew louder every time I watched TV and saw teenagers living lives I could only imagine.Dreams of comfort.

Dreams of freedom.Dreams of leaving the province.Dreams of working, earning, and building a life where I didn't have to ask permission to breathe.Dreams of becoming someone who could take care of herself — and maybe, one day, take care of everyone else too.

And so I did achieve my dream — at least the first step of it. After finishing high school, I earned a scholarship to one of the best schools in Davao City, run by nuns: The University of the Immaculate Conception. I wanted to take up Bachelor of Science in Accountancy, but my mother chose Nursing for me. Back then, Nursing was the most popular course because it offered the chance to go abroad and help your family. I didn't want that course, but I said yes.

My mother told me, "You have to be a nurse so you

can send money to us and make us rich." I said, "I don't want to be rich," and she replied, "Yes you do, because I told you. You do whatever I say! It is best for you and our family. You should be grateful that I let you go to college and not let you work for the rest of your life." Those were the lines she always reminded me. It hurts a little bit. I felt my achievements weren't even recognized or why should I do the things I don'twant to? or why I should be the one lifting our family from rags?

I remember after high school, I asked her if I could enroll in college, and she said, "What for? Why don't you just marry? Our job is done and I'm tired having conversations about that." But I insisted to her that I finished with honors and had a scholarship. So I spoke with my father instead, and he said, "Yes, you can go to college — but promise me you'll be a rich kid someday, so I can live the life I wanted." Those were his words. They don't care what I could be someday. All it matters to them what I could bring in the table for them. I guess every breadwinner in the family understands that now. It is a very sad truth. But I never complained or thought any other way at that time. My only concern was that I finally had a chance to build myself, to gain freedom away from the province. I was celebrating quietly inside — finally, I could be on my own.

This time, I felt about recognising the first signs of being a breadwinner in the family —the responsibilities,the expectations,the dreams,the quiet strength —that would eventually lead me there.

I didn't choose the role. But I grew into it. And it began —in the province, in the silence, in the small moments that taught me how to carry a family long before I carried my own life.

CHAPTER 9
LEAVING THE PROVINCE AND ENTERING A NEW WORLD

Leaving the province felt like stepping out of a cage I didn't know I was trapped in. For years, my world had been shaped by rules, responsibilities, and the weight of other people's expectations. But now, for the first time, I was stepping into something that felt like mine — even if it wasn't perfect, even if it wasn't exactly the path I wanted.

I still remember the day I left.No dramatic goodbye.No tears.
Just a quiet determination inside me, whispering, This is your chance.

I carried my old travelling bag — the same one my father loved, the same one that held our lives when we moved to the province. But this time, it held something different: hope. A small, trembling hope that maybe, just maybe, life could be bigger than what I had known.

I had earned a scholarship to one of the best schools in Davao City, the University of the Immaculate Conception, run by nuns. I wanted to take up Accountancy — numbers made sense to me, and I dreamed of becoming someone who could build a life with stability and dignity. But my mother chose Nursing for me and so my father did. Back then, Nursing was the golden ticket.The course that promised a job abroad.The course that promised money.The course that promised a way out — not for me, but for my family.

   Leaving wasn't just about education.It was about escape.It was about possibility.It was about finally breathing without asking permission.

   When I stepped onto the bus to Davao City, I felt something shift inside me.A quiet celebration.A small victory.A whisper of the woman I would one day become.For the first time in my life, I wasn't just surviving.I was beginning.

   I felt sad about leaving them — my friends, my family, my brother — but a bigger part of me wanted to be on my own and experience life beyond the province. Some people smiled at me proudly, wishing me well, but most of them — including relatives and neighbours — had already made their judgment. They whispered that I would end up coming back home, that I wouldn't finish college, that I would get pregnant, that I would end up just like anybody else in town. Their words stung, not because they were true, but because they believed them so easily.

   I was a little scared of their judgment, but as a teenager, the strongest feeling I knew was rebellion — that fire inside you that rises whenever someone doubts you or tries to control your future. I felt angry at them, angry at their assumptions, angry at how small they thought my life would be. And I told myself quietly, One day, when I come back to this city, I will show them they were wrong.

So I left with that fire inside me, thinking about what my life would be like out there. I imagined who I would meet, what kind of person I would become. In my mind, everything felt easy, simple, exciting — like stepping into a dream I had been building for years. I didn't know yet that life outside the province held its own hardships, its own dangers, its own lessons I never expected.

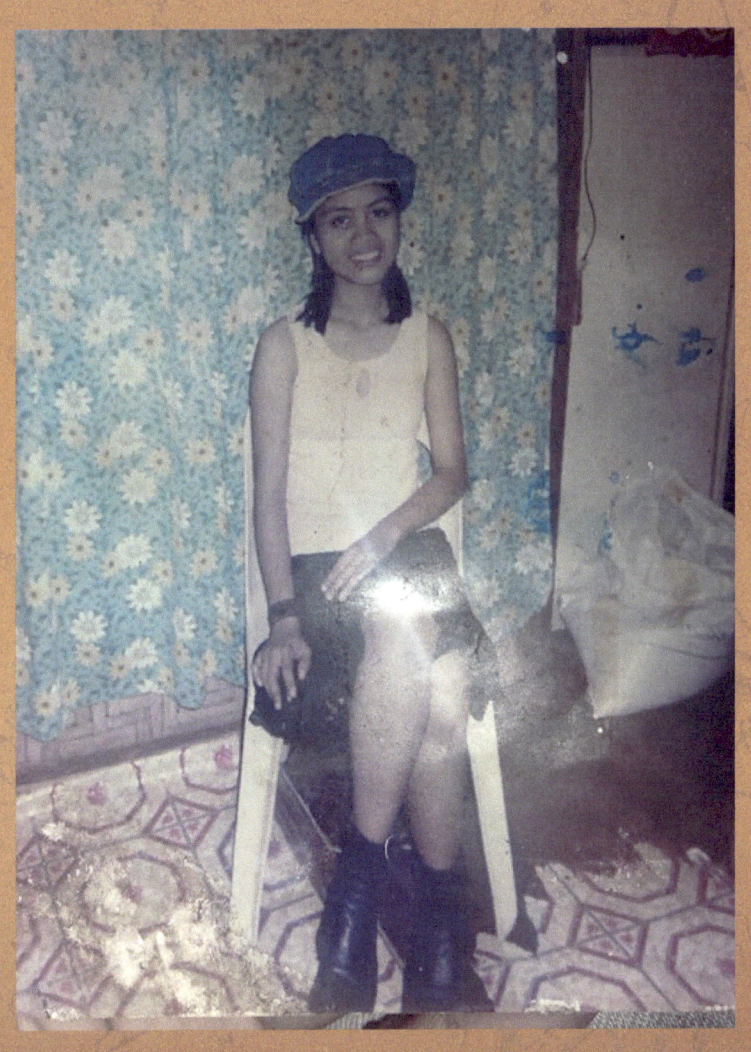

CHAPTER 10
LIFE IN THE CITY: FREEDOM, FEAR, AND FINDING MYSELF

The city greeted me with noise — a kind of noise I wasn't used to. Cars honking, people rushing, vendors shouting, jeepneys stopping and going like they had no brakes. It was overwhelming, but in a strange way, it felt alive. It felt like possibility. It felt like the world I had only imagined under the dim light of a lampara.

For the first time, I wasn't waking up to roosters or the sound of people walking to the farm. I wasn't sweeping the yard before sunrise. I wasn't being watched by neighbours who counted every move I made. I wasn't being told who I could talk to or what I should avoid.

I was in the city.And the city didn't know me.The city didn't judge me.The city didn't care about my past. That alone felt like freedom.But freedom, I learned quickly, came with fear.
I didn't know how to navigate jeepneys.I didn't know how to cross busy streets.I didn't know how to talk to strangers without feeling like I was breaking a rule.I didn't know how to live without someone telling me what to do.

I was excited — but I was also terrified.

The University of the Immaculate Conception was bigger than any school I had ever seen. The nuns walked with quiet authority, the students looked confident, and the hallways felt like they belonged to people who already knew who they were. I felt small. I felt out of place. Bangkerohan, a suburban part of Davao City, where my University is located, was the first place that truly shocked my senses. It was nothing like the quiet mornings of the province. The moment I stepped into Davao City, Bangkerohan greeted me with its own kind of chaos — the kind that felt alive, loud, and unstoppable. Vendors lined the streets selling fruits, vegetables, fish, and anything you could imagine.

The air smelled of durian mixed with the scent of fresh produce and the smoke from street food grills. Jeepneys honked endlessly, tricycles weaved through crowds, and people moved fast, like they were always late for something. The market never seemed to sleep. It was noisy, messy, colourful, and overwhelming — but it was also full of life.

For someone who grew up waking to roosters and the sound of people walking to the farm, Bangkerohan felt like another universe. It was the first place that made me realise I wasn't in the province anymore. I wasn't in a world where everyone knew me, watched me, or judged me. Here, I was just another face in the crowd — and that alone again felt like freedom or a bird out in the cage.

But I also felt determined. I didn't come all the way from the province to prove the gossipers right. I didn't leave my family to fail. I didn't fight for my education just to go home defeated. So I pushed myself. I woke up early.I studied hard.I learned how to navigate jeepney routes.I learned how to budget my allowance.I learned how to survive in a world that didn't slow down for anyone.But the city wasn't just about school.It was about discovering who I was outside the expectations of my family.

I learned how to laugh without fear of being judged.I learned how to make friends who didn't know my past.I learned how to speak without worrying about gossip.I learned how to dream bigger than the life I left behind.

But I also learned how dangerous the world could be.There were nights I walked home scared.Days when money wasn't enough.Moments when loneliness hit me harder than any responsibility in the province ever did.Times when I questioned if I made the right choice.Times when I wanted to go home but refused to because I didn't want to prove anyone right.

The city taught me independence — but it also taught me survival.I learned to trust my instincts.I learned to protect myself.I learned that freedom wasn't just about doing what you want — it was about carrying the consequences of your choices.

And slowly, I began to change.I wasn't the quiet girl from the province anymore.I wasn't the child who followed every rule.
I wasn't the girl who feared gossip or judgment.I was becoming someone else — someone stronger, someone braver, someone who could stand on her own.

The city didn't just give me freedom.It gave me identity.It gave me courage.It gave me the first real taste of the woman I was becoming.

When I first entered my dormitory — before I ever moved in with my aunt or any relatives — I stayed in a girls' dorm just across from my university, right where the nuns lived.

I shared a small room with another student. She was pretty, kind, and welcoming, and the landlady treated me gently too. But even with their warmth, I realised how difficult it was for me to talk to anyone. I was shy, scared, unsure of myself, but I didn't let it stop me. My school had strict rules — stricter than anything I had ever experienced.

Our uniforms were monitored carefully: skirts never above the knee, hair neatly tied, faces clean. No makeup. No hair colour. No high heels — only black shoes. And if the lady guard saw you wearing a coloured bra under your very white "gala" uniform. It is the formal, all-white uniform worn by nursing students in the Philippines. It's the kind of uniform that makes you stand straighter the moment you put it on.

The fabric is bright white — so white that even the slightest shadow or coloured undergarment becomes visible. The skirt falls below the knee, crisp and pressed, and the top is structured with a clean collar and fitted sleeves. Everything about it demands neatness, discipline, and purity. If you are spotted smoething coloured within you wouldn't be allowed to enter.

If you insisted, you'd end up in the dean's office — the highest nun in the school. It was a different world of discipline and expectations. My days started at 7 a.m. and ended at 3 or 4 p.m., and my life became a routine of school, dormitory, school, dormitory. It was new, overwhelming, and lonely at times — but I chose that routine because it felt safe.

Then I met people, especially my roommate. I will never forget her. She was the one who helped me explore what the city truly was. And just like that, my life in the city began.

CHAPTER 11
THE STRUGGLES OF NURSING SCHOOL

Nursing school was nothing like I imagined. It wasn't just about wearing a white uniform and learning how to take care of people. It was discipline. It was pressure.

It was a test of who you were — and who you were becoming.
The first weeks felt like stepping into a world that demanded perfection. Every morning, I woke up before sunrise, fixing my uniform, making sure my hair was tied neatly, checking that my shoes were polished. The nuns didn't tolerate even the smallest mistake. A wrinkle on your skirt, a loose strand of hair, a coloured bra under your gala — any of these could send you straight to the dean's office. It felt like every day was an inspection, not just of your appearance, but of your character.

"I struggled at first.
 Not because I wasn't capable, but because I didn't choose this path.
 I was studying for a dream that wasn't mine."

Nursing wasn't really my dream course, but I still pushed myself to stay on top — especially to be in the Dean's List and to be recognized as one of the best student nurses in different areas. Well, not in everything. I was more inclined to the Delivery Room and the Pediatrics Department. Those were the places where I felt a little more alive, a little more connected. But it was hard — memorizing all the medical terms, pretending to love subjects that didn't spark joy in me, carrying huge books that felt heavier than my own doubts. Still, I had no choice. I had to survive the course chosen for me, even if my heart belonged somewhere else.

Inside the classroom, the pressure was even heavier.Nursing wasn't just memorization — it was precision.It was responsibility.It was life and death.I was studying for a dream that wasn't mine.

While my classmates talked excitedly about becoming nurses, going abroad, earning dollars, helping their families, I sat quietly, wondering if I belonged there. I wanted to take Accountancy. I wanted numbers, logic, structure. But instead, I was learning anatomy, pharmacology, and procedures that made my hands shake.

There were days I cried silently in the dormitory, afraid to show weakness.Days when I felt stupid.Days when I felt lost.Days when I questioned if I made the right choice — or if I even had a choice at all.But I kept going.Because going home wasn't an option.Because proving people wrong mattered.Because I wanted freedom more than anything.

My roommate became my first real friend in the city. She was confident, outgoing, and unafraid — everything I wasn't. She taught me how to navigate jeepneys, where to buy cheap food, how to survive the city without looking scared. She showed me that life outside the province could be fun, even if it was hard.

With her, I learned how to laugh again.

But even with friendship, Nursing school was relentless.Exams came one after another.Quizzes every day.Skills check-offs that made your heart race.Clinical duties that required you to be alert, calm, and perfect — even when you were trembling inside.

I remember my first time in the hospital.The smell of antiseptic.The coldness of the floors.The sound of patients coughing, crying, calling for help.I felt like a child pretending to be an adult.

But I also felt something else — something I didn't expect.I felt needed.For the first time, I understood why people chose Nursing.It wasn't just about going abroad.It wasn't just about money.It was about being there for someone who couldn't help themselves.It was about giving comfort.It was about being trusted.

And slowly, I began to grow into the role.Not because it was my dream, but because I learned how to survive anything placed in front of me. Nursing school didn't just teach me medical skills.It taught me resilience.It taught me discipline.It taught me how to stand on my own even when I was shaking.

Looking back now, I realise that my life then wasn't about becoming a nurse.It was about becoming stronger.It was about learning how to fight for myself.It was about discovering that even when life gives you a path you didn't choose, you can still walk it with courage.Nursing school didn't break me.It built me.Quietly.Painfully. Beautifully.

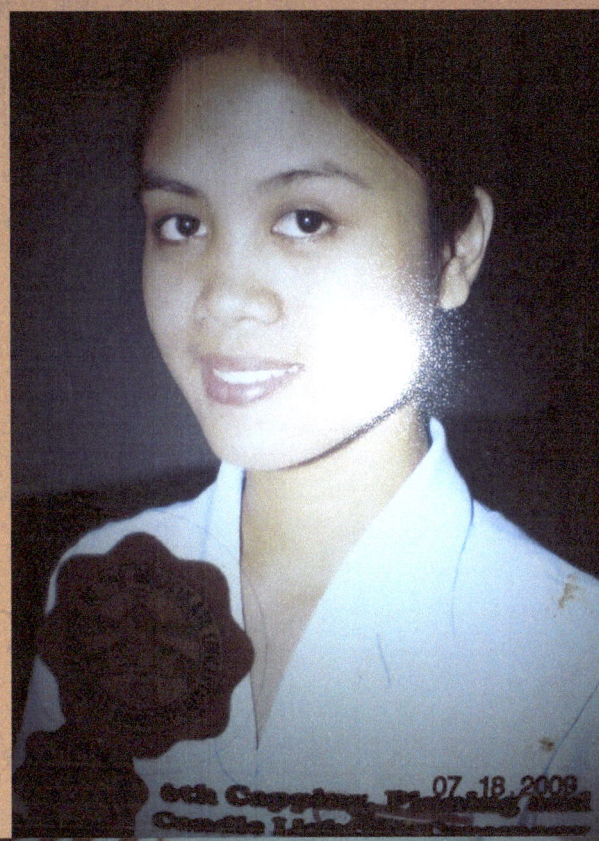
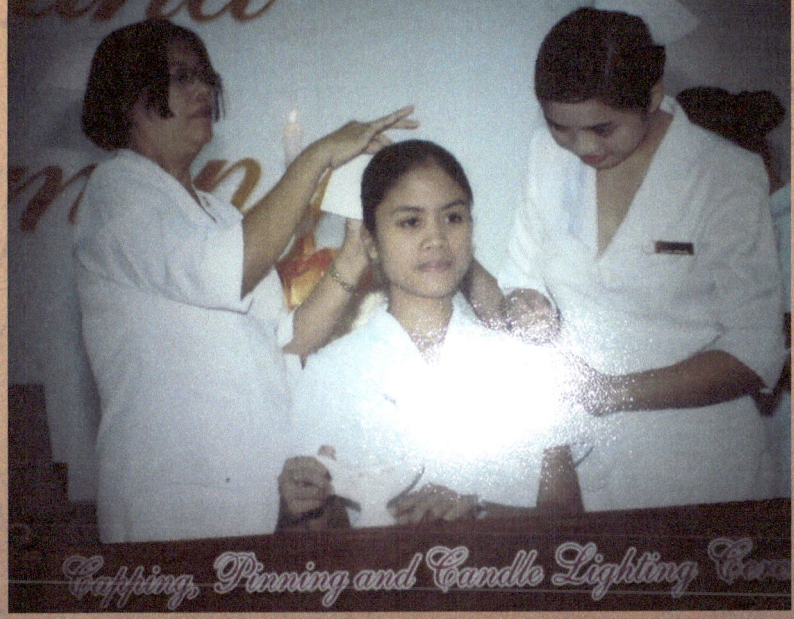

CHAPTER 12
THE LONELINESS THAT FOLLOWED

People think that once you leave home, freedom feels like a celebration.And in the beginning, it did.But freedom also has a shadow — a quiet, heavy one — and that shadow is loneliness.

After the excitement of the city settled, after the noise of the city became familiar, after the routine of school and dormitory felt normal, something else began to creep in. It wasn't fear. It wasn't regret. It was a kind of emptiness I didn't know how to name.I missed home.Not the rules.Not the gossip.Not the expectations.But the familiarity — the feeling of belonging somewhere, even if that place was heavy.

In the city, no one knew me.No one knew my story.No one knew my family.No one knew the girl who grew up sweeping yards, running errands, and reading under a lampara.And sometimes, being unknown felt like freedom.But other times, it felt like disappearing.

There were nights in the dormitory when the silence felt too loud. My roommate would be out with friends, exploring the city, laughing, living. And I would sit on my bed, staring at my books, pretending I was fine. Pretending I wasn't lonely. Pretending I didn't feel like a stranger in my own life.I didn't know how to tell anyone that I was struggling.I didn't know how to say I felt lost.I didn't know how to ask for help.In the province, you didn't talk about feelings.You just survived them.So I survived.

I buried myself in schoolwork.I memorized medical terms until my head hurt.I studied late into the night, hoping the exhaustion would drown the loneliness.I walked the hallways with confidence I didn't feel.I smiled when people talked to me, even when my chest felt tight.

But loneliness has a way of finding you, even in crowded places.There were days when I felt invisible.Days when I felt like I didn't belong anywhere — not in the province, not in the city, not even in the life I was trying to build.Days when I wondered if I made a mistake leaving home.Days when I wanted to run back, but pride held me still.And yet, in that loneliness, something unexpected happened.

I began to know myself.Not the girl shaped by rules.Not the girl shaped by expectations.Not the girl shaped by fear of gossip or judgment.But the girl who could sit with her own thoughts.The girl who could comfort herself.The girl who could survive without anyone telling her what to do.Loneliness taught me resilience.It taught me independence.It taught me how to stand on my own without collapsing.It taught me that freedom isn't loud — sometimes it's quiet, painful, and earned in silence.As time past by, I slowly realise that my life wasn't about being alone.It was about learning how to be with myself.It was about discovering that even in the emptiest moments, I had strength I didn't know existed.Loneliness didn't break me.It shaped me.It carved out space inside me for the woman I was becoming —a woman who could endure,a woman who could rise,a woman who could walk through the world without losing herself.

CHAPTER 13
THE CHALLENGES THAT TESTED ME

Life in the city wasn't just about freedom or loneliness.It was about the challenges that came one after another — challenges that tested my patience, my courage, and my sense of self. Some days, it felt like the city was a teacher, giving me lessons I didn't ask for but desperately needed.

The first challenge was survival.Not the dramatic kind — but the quiet, everyday survival that no one talks about.Budgeting my allowance.Stretching a few pesos to last a week.Choosing between buying food or photocopying notes.Walking long distances because jeepney fare was too much.Pretending I wasn't hungry when my stomach was empty.In the province, we didn't have much, but at least we had food.In the city, everything had a price.

The second challenge was academics.Nursing wasn't my dream, but I pushed myself to excel anyway. I forced myself to memorize medical terms that felt like another language. I carried thick books that felt heavier than my own doubts. I stayed up late studying, not because I loved the course, but because I refused to fail. I wanted to stay in the Dean's List. I wanted to be recognized as one of the best student nurses in the areas I loved — especially the Delivery Room and Pediatrics. Those departments made me feel connected, purposeful, even if the rest of the course didn't.

But it was exhausting.Every quiz felt like a judgment.Every clinical duty felt like a test of my worth.Every mistake felt like a reminder that this wasn't the life I chose.The third challenge was people.The city was full of them — loud, confident, fast-moving people who seemed to know exactly who they were. I didn't. I was still learning how to speak without fear, how to make friends without feeling like I was breaking a rule, how to trust people who didn't grow up with the same values I did.Some people were kind.Some were curious.Some were dangerous. I learned quickly that not everyone who smiled at you had good intentions.I learned to protect myself.I learned to say no.I learned to walk away.

It is one of the biggest challenges I faced because I was just learning how to meet and talk to new people. At first, I was shy and guarded, but loneliness has a way of pushing you toward anyone who offers comfort. When I started talking to classmates who eventually became friends, it felt like a new life was opening up for me. I was so hungry for connection, for belonging, for company, that I didn't stop to check whether these people were genuine or not. As long as I wasn't alone, as long as I felt part of a group, I welcomed anyone into my world. Little did I know how much influence they would have on me. Slowly, I started partying, drinking alcohol, and skipping classes. I thought I was finally living the life I used to imagine — carefree, fun, exciting. I was happy at first, or at least I convinced myself I was. But later, I realised it was a big mistake, one that pulled me further away from the person I wanted to become.

The fourth challenge was homesickness.Even when I didn't want to go back to the province, there were moments when I missed the familiarity — the sound of my brother's laughter, the smell of home-cooked food, the comfort of knowing exactly where I belonged. In the city, I belonged everywhere and nowhere at the same time.But the hardest challenge of all was identity. Who was I without my family's expectations?Who was I without the province's rules?Who was I when no one was watching?Who was I becoming?

There were days when I felt strong — like I could conquer anything.And there were days when I felt like a little girl pretending to be brave. But every challenge, every hardship, every tear I hid in the dormitory shaped me.They taught me resilience.They taught me independence.They taught me that strength isn't loud — sometimes it's quiet, steady, and built in the moments no one sees.

One thing I realise is that my life wasn't about suffering.It was about transformation.It was about learning how to stand tall even when everything around me felt uncertain.It was about discovering that I could survive more than I ever imagined.

The challenges didn't break me.They prepared me.For the woman I was becoming.For the life I would build.For the future I was determined to claim — no matter how hard the journey would be.

CHAPTER 14
FRIENDSHIPS THAT SAVED ME

After everything I had gone through — the loneliness, the pressure of Nursing school, the mistakes I made trying to fit in — I didn't expect that friendship would be the thing that pulled me back to myself. But it did. Not all friendships, of course. Some were temporary, born from convenience and loneliness. But a few... a few were real. And those few changed everything.

It didn't happen all at once. It started quietly, in the small moments — a shared laugh, a borrowed pen, a classmate waiting for me after duty, someone offering to walk with me to the dormitory. These were simple gestures, but they felt like lifelines. After months of feeling invisible, I finally felt seen.

The first real friendships I made weren't loud or dramatic. They were gentle and steady. They were the kind of friendships that didn't demand anything from me except honesty. These were the people who didn't care where I came from, what my family was like, or how strict my upbringing had been. They didn't judge my accent, my clothes, or my shyness. They accepted me as I was — a girl trying to survive a life she didn't choose. They didn't know it, but they were saving me. They saved me from the loneliness that had been eating me alive. They saved me from the wrong crowd I had fallen into. They saved me from the version of myself I was becoming — the one who partied too much, drank too much, skipped classes, and pretended she was okay.

These new friends were different. They were focused. They were kind. They were grounded. They were the kind of people who reminded me of the girl I used to be — the girl who studied under a lampara, who dreamed of a better life, who believed she could rise above her circumstances. Slowly, I began to change again. Not because they forced me to, but because being around them made me want to be better. They helped me study. They encouraged me when I felt overwhelmed. They listened when I finally opened up about my struggles. They reminded me that I wasn't alone — not anymore. And for the first time since leaving the province, I felt something I hadn't felt in a long time: **belonging.** These friendships didn't erase the challenges. They didn't magically fix my life. But they gave me strength. They gave me stability. They gave me a reason to keep going. I realised that life wasn't about finding the people who reflected the best parts of me — the parts I thought I had lost. It was about learning that not everyone comes into your life to break you. Some come to build you. Some come to guide you. Some come to remind you of who you are. These friendships didn't just save me. They shaped me. They helped me grow into the woman I was becoming —a woman who could choose better, love better, and trust herself again. But even though they helped me, for me, it was already too late. A tragedy — something unexpected — happened. I found out I was pregnant, and in that moment, everything changed. My identity shifted. My friendships shifted. The girl I was, the girl I was becoming, the girl my friends knew — she all changed in an instant. My life took a turn I never imagined, and nothing would ever be the same again.

CHAPTER 15
THE MOMENT EVERYTHING CHANGED

Pregnancy was never part of my plan. Not at that age. Not in that moment of my life. Not when I was still trying to understand who I was in the city. But life doesn't wait for you to be ready. Sometimes it just happens — quietly, suddenly, and without asking permission.

When I found out I was pregnant, I felt everything at once: fear, shock, confusion, and strangely... a small spark of excitement I couldn't explain. I wasn't ready, but a part of me already loved the tiny life growing inside me. Still, I hid it. I hid it from everyone — my teachers, my classmates, my friends, even from myself sometimes. I hid my pregnancy for almost seven months.

Every day became a performance. Every outfit was chosen to hide my belly. Every movement was calculated. Every step outside felt like a risk. I was terrified that someone from the province would see me, recognise me, and report everything to my parents. The shame, the gossip, the judgment — I could already hear it. I could already feel it. So I kept quiet. I kept small. I kept hidden.

But even in my fear, abortion never crossed my mind. Not once. Some of my college friends had gone through it — scared of their parents, scared of their future, scared of the consequences. I understood their fear, but my heart couldn't go there. I knew I had to protect the life inside me, no matter how unprepared I was. So I did what I could. I took vitamins. I ate healthy food when I could afford it. I forced myself to rest even when my mind was racing. I went to hospital duties even when I felt nauseated, dizzy, and weak.

I remember standing in the ward, pretending to be fine while my body felt like it was collapsing. My friends noticed something was off — the way I moved, the way I breathed, the way I held my stomach without realising it. They kept asking, "Are you okay?" in a tone that felt different, almost suspicious. But they never pushed. They just watched me with quiet concern.

And then came the day I could no longer hide. My mother called me on a prepaid line. Her voice was calm, but I felt my whole body shaking. She asked how I was, and I lied — "I'm fine." But my voice trembled. She paused, then said something that made my heart stop. "I had a dream," she said. "A stroller. A baby. It was strange."

My breath caught. My hands went cold. I dropped the phone.
Then she said the words I feared most: "I will visit you there."

Panic swallowed me whole. I cried so hard I couldn't breathe. I didn't know what to say, what to do, where to go. So I ran. For two days, I disappeared. No calls. No messages. No explanations.

I didn't know that my mother had already arrived in the city.I didn't know she was calling the police.I didn't know she was asking everyone who knew me where I was.I didn't know she was searching for me like a missing person.When I finally returned, exhausted and terrified, I saw her waiting.Her face was a mix of anger, fear, and disappointment. I lifted my shirt and showed her my belly — the truth I had been hiding for months.Her reaction cut through me like a blade.She was furious.She was heartbroken.She told me I was a disgrace to the family.

And in that moment, everything changed — my life, my identity, my future.The girl I had been was gone.The woman I needed to become had no choice but to rise.

The moment my mother saw my belly, everything inside me shattered.Her face — the shock, the anger, the disappointment — burned itself into my memory.I had imagined this moment a thousand times, but nothing prepared me for the real thing.

She didn't speak softly.She didn't cry.She didn't ask if I was okay.She called me a disgrace.A humiliation.An embarrassment to the family.And even though her words cut deep, I understood where they came from — fear, shame, and the weight of a culture that judged women harshly for mistakes men walked away from freely. But understanding didn't make it hurt any less.

In that moment, I felt small.Smaller than I had ever felt in my life.Smaller than the girl who grew up sweeping yards and following rules. Smaller than the teenager who left the province with hope in her heart. I felt like I had failed everyone — my family, my friends, myself. But beneath the shame, something else was growing. Something quiet. Something steady. Something strong. I wasn't just carrying a child. I was carrying a new version of myself.

The aftermath wasn't easy. My mother's anger didn't fade overnight. The disappointment in her eyes followed me everywhere. The silence between us felt heavier than any words she could have said. I felt judged even when no one was looking. I felt dirty even when I was clean. I felt unworthy even when I tried to forgive myself.

But I also felt determined. I knew I had to survive — not just for me, but for the life inside me. I knew I had to be strong — even when I felt weak. I knew I had to keep going — even when everything around me felt like it was falling apart.

The shame was real, but so was the strength that grew from it. I learned how to endure the whispers. I learned how to ignore the stares. I learned how to walk with my head up even when my heart was breaking. I learned that survival isn't always loud or heroic. Sometimes it's quiet. Sometimes it's lonely. Sometimes it's just waking up every day and choosing to keep going.

My friends didn't know how to react. Some drifted away. Some stayed but didn't know what to say. Some tried to comfort me, but I could feel the distance growing. I wasn't the same girl anymore. And they didn't know how to hold the new version of me.

But even in the loneliness, I found strength. Strength in my body as it changed. Strength in my heart as it softened. Strength in my mind as it accepted the truth. I was going to be a mother. Whether I was ready or not. Whether people approved or not. Whether my family forgave me or not. The aftermath of my pregnancy wasn't just about shame. It was about transformation.

It was about discovering a strength I didn't know I had. It was about surviving a storm I never expected to face. It was the beginning of everything —the beginning of responsibility, the beginning of courage, the beginning of a love that would change me forever.

So I went back to town and stopped school during the last two months before my graduation in Nursing. I felt broken, depressed, and completely lost. People stared at me like I was a scandal walking through the streets. The gossip spread faster than I could breathe.

My father turned into a wild beast — angry, disappointed, wounded. He told me I was nobody, that I was just like anyone else who allowed a man to ruin everything. I could see he was broken too, but not because of my situation — because of the shame, the judgment, the whispers from people and relatives. I felt like everyone was angry at me, unable to accept what had happened. I cried all the time, drowning in emotions I didn't know how to carry. But somehow, my strength was louder than my pain. I was never ashamed of being pregnant — not because of anything I learned in Nursing school, but because I knew I had no choice now.

I never questioned God about what happened to me, but I was disappointed — not with the baby I was carrying, not with the father, but because I never had the chance to explain myself. I never even had a boyfriend, and suddenly there I was, pregnant. I tried to forget the details of what exactly happened to me. My identity and personality had always pushed me to move forward, to leave the past behind because you can't change it. It was easy to think that way, but living it was different. The process was painful — enduring the
physical changes, the emotional storms, the joy and fear of pregnancy, and the constant questions from people who treated my life like the latest news in town. It was hard. I had to be strong for myself and for the little one growing inside me, even though I had no idea how to be a parent. I had to be strong for myself and for the little one growing inside me, even though I had no idea how to be a parent.

And even in the middle of all that pain, judgment, and confusion, a small voice inside me whispered that this was not the end of my story — it was the beginning of the woman I was meant to become.

CHAPTER 17
BECOMING A MOTHER AT A YOUNG AGE

The days after my mother found out felt like walking through a storm with no umbrella.Everything was loud — the shouting, the gossip, the disappointment — yet inside me, everything was quiet. Too quiet. Like my heart was holding its breath, waiting for something to break.But nothing broke.Not me.Not the baby.Not the tiny thread of strength I was holding onto.I didn't know how to be a mother.I didn't even know how to be an adult.But life didn't wait for me to figure it out.

My belly grew.My world shrank.And every day, I felt myself changing — not because I wanted to, but because I had to.The shame around me was suffocating.People stared like I was a walking warning.Relatives whispered like my life was a scandal they needed to dissect.Neighbours looked at me with pity, curiosity, or disgust — never kindness.

But inside me, something else was growing besides the baby.A quiet, stubborn strength.A strength that whispered, You can do this.I was young, scared, and unprepared — but I wasn't weak.I learned how to endure the questions that felt like knives."Who's the father?""What happened to you?""Why did you ruin your life?"

People asked like they had the right to know, like my pain was entertainment.I learned how to ignore the stares that followed me everywhere.I learned how to walk with my head up even when my heart felt heavy.I learned how to protect my baby from the world long before I ever held them in my arms.My father's anger was the hardest to carry.He didn't see my fear.He didn't see my confusion.He didn't see the girl who had never even had a boyfriend, suddenly pregnant and trying to understand her own story.He only saw shame.Shame from the town.Shame from relatives.Shame from the expectations I had shattered.He told me I was nobody.That I had allowed a man to ruin everything.

But deep inside, I knew something he didn't:I wasn't ruined.I was transforming.I never questioned God about what happened to me.But I was disappointed — not in the baby, not in the father, but in the fact that I never had the chance to explain myself.I never had the chance to say what really happened.I never had the chance to defend the girl I used to be.So I did what I always did:I moved forward.

My personality had always been shaped by survival — forgetting what you can't change, accepting what you can't undo, and focusing on what's coming next.It sounded simple, but living it was painful. Pregnancy was not easy.The nausea.The dizziness.The sleepless nights.The emotional storms.The joy and fear tangled together.The constant questions from people who treated my life like the latest headline.

But through all of it, I held on.I held on for the baby who didn't ask to be here.I held on for the future I still wanted to build.I held on for the woman I was slowly becoming.Becoming a mother at a young age didn't break me.It reshaped me.It carved out a deeper strength, a deeper love, a deeper understanding of who I was meant to be.And even though the world around me was loud with judgment, inside me there was a quiet truth growing stronger every day:This child was not my downfall.This child was my beginning.

And on August 6, 2010, I gave birth to a beautiful baby girl. I named her **Alhan Farisha** — an Arabic name that means Holy Hope. And she truly was my hope. My world. The moment I held her, something inside me shifted forever. I felt strong, and somehow even stronger than before. I knew I could endure any pain, any judgment, any hardship, just to protect her. She changed everything — the way I saw myself, the way I understood my life, and the way I needed to be. In her tiny hands, I found a new purpose. In her first cry, I found a new version of myself.

Having her brought a feeling so deep I still struggle to put it into words. It was a mix of wonder, fear, and a love so fierce it almost hurt. I was terrified of how I would raise her — especially knowing I couldn't depend on anyone, not even her father. But at the same time, something inside me began to expand. I started dreaming bigger, not for myself alone, but for her. She became the root of every dream, every hope, every quiet prayer I whispered at night. My purpose shifted. My life was no longer just about surviving — it was about building a future for the little girl who had suddenly become my whole world.And slowly, without even realising it, she became the reason I would rise again. The reason I would work harder, dream louder, and push myself beyond every limit placed on me. She became the button to start myself as a breadwinner I would become — the woman who would carry not just her own life, but the lives of the people she loved. In her tiny presence, I found the strength to imagine a future where I could provide, protect, and lead. She didn't just change my life. She became the fire that would guide every step I took from that moment on.

Becoming a mother at a young age taught me lessons I never imagined I would learn so early. I remember whispering to my daughter, even when she was just days old, that I would give her everything — a life filled with comfort, safety, and the freedom to be herself. I didn't want her to grow up the way I did. Not because I hated my childhood, but because I knew it wasn't the kind of life I wanted for her. I wanted her to feel loved without fear, understood without judgment, and guided with a gentle voice. I knew it wouldn't be easy, but I believed I could do it.

I started working part time jobs early, like selling items, foods , very determined to prove to everyone — and to myself — that I could still be a responsible mother. But people looked down on me, even my own family. There wasn't a day when I didn't hear an insult, a reminder that they thought I had ruined my life. My father and mother doubted me. My brother, in a moment of anger, screamed in my face that I was just like "other girls who opened their legs and became a disgrace." He said I would be an obligation, that I would never be able to help the family. Nobody believed in me. Nobody saw me. Only God knew the truth of what I was carrying — the real me, the pain I hid, the battles I fought in silence.

There were moments when the weight of their words crushed me so deeply that I wondered if ending everything would finally make the pain stop. I cried until my chest hurt, hoping something — anything — would get better. But even in that darkness, I kept going. I woke up at night to carry my crying baby, fed her, bathed her, washed her tiny clothes with my tired hands. My mother helped a little, but she also wanted me to struggle, to learn how hard motherhood truly was. And I did learn — through exhaustion, through tears, through love that refused to die.

I took my daughter to the health center for her vaccinations by myself without any help, walking kilometers and passing by neighbors and people whom I belived are gossipping about me. I bought things only for her not in department stores cause I can't afford it that time. I bought it in "ukay-ukay" and guess what? I remembered my childhood days pf doing that with my mother. I don't feel sad but I have been motivated more with myself and poured every bit of my energy into her future.

My world revolved around her — there was nothing else I could think about except the life I wanted her to have. As time passed, I realised how hard it truly was. While she slept at night, I would rush to my evening classes because I had enrolled myself in another course. I wanted to prove to people — and to myself — that I could still achieve something, even if it was far from

Nursing. I took Financial Management, something closer to the Accountancy course I once dreamed of. People at school understood and respected me as a young mother. They were younger than me, yet they showed me so much kindness and consideration, especially my teachers.

To support myself and my daughter, I sold anything I could — perfumes, dresses, food packs, small items. And they bought them. Thank God. It made me realise that all those years of selling in elementary school were not a burden but a blessing. They taught me resilience, confidence, and the ability to survive. For three years, I juggled motherhood, studies, and selling — and I graduated. I actually graduated. The joy I felt was something words could never fully capture.

Two months before graduation, I was accepted into a job at a travel agency, booking flights and ship tickets, both domestic and international. I felt lucky, blessed, and seen. I told my parents about it, and my mother didn't say a word. She just continued cooking, acting as if she hadn't heard anything — but I knew deep inside she was proud. On graduation day, people in town watched me walk in my toga, wearing medals and ribbons. But honestly, none of that mattered to me. What mattered was that I had finally proven something — not to them, but to myself. I rose above the look-downs, the judgments, the whispers. I achieved one of my dreams, and I did it while carrying the weight of the world and the love of a child who became my purpose.

And in that moment, I finally realised I was never alone in this kind of battle. As I looked around during graduation, I saw other students wearing the same toga, carrying their own children. I had always thought I was the only one living this kind of story — but I wasn't. Life has a way of making you believe your pain is unique, but when you open your eyes and step outside your own world, you see that others are fighting their own silent wars too. You realise there is beauty beyond the struggle, and that no matter how heavy your burden feels, you are never the only one carrying it.

My victory became an eye-opener for many in town — especially young mothers, my cousins, and people who once doubted me. They saw that dreams are still possible if you want them badly enough, if you stay focused, determined, and willing to persevere through the pain.

Being a young mother, being poor, being judged — none of it is a hindrance to the life you want to build. From that moment, I started receiving people's applause. I felt respect growing around me, as if I had won something big. At first, I thought it was just because I graduated from college — something not many cared about before. But no, it wasn't just the diploma. It was the fact that I endured the insults, the "panlalait," the shame, and still rose above it all without abandoning my responsibilities to my daughter or my mother. That was the real victory — not the medals, not the ribbons, but the strength it took to survive and rise.

My victory became an eye-opener for many in town — especially young mothers, my cousins, and people who once doubted me. They saw that dreams are still possible if you want them badly enough, if you stay focused, determined, and willing to persevere through the pain. Being a young mother, being poor, being judged — none of it is a hindrance to the life you want to build. From that moment, I started receiving people's applause. I felt respect growing around me, as if I had won something big.

At first, I thought it was just because I graduated from college — something not many cared about before. But no, it wasn't just the diploma. It was the fact that I endured the insults or "panlalait," the shame, and still rose above it all without abandoning my responsibilities to my daughter or my mother. That was the real victory — not the medals, not the ribbons, but the strength it took to survive and rise.

CHAPTER 18
THE RISE OF MY RESPONSIBILITIES

Graduation wasn't the end of my struggles — it was the beginning of a new kind of battle. A battle that didn't involve shame or judgment anymore, but responsibility. Real responsibility. The kind that wakes you up before sunrise and keeps you moving long after your body wants to rest.

The moment I stepped out of school, I stepped into work. Not just one job — but many. Because I didn't have the luxury of choosing only one path. I had a daughter to raise, a family to help, and a future to build from scratch.

My first job at the travel agency felt like a blessing. I booked flights and ship tickets, answered calls, handled customers, and learned how to deal with people from all walks of life. It wasn't glamorous, but it was honest work — and it was mine. Every peso I earned felt like a small victory, a quiet reminder that I was capable of more than people believed.

But one job wasn't enough.

After work, I sold perfumes, dresses, food packs, anything I could carry in a bag. I walked from office to office, classroom to classroom, offering items with a smile even when my feet were aching. I learned how to negotiate, how to market, how to talk to people with confidence. I learned how to survive.

And when I got home, I wasn't done.I was a mother again — feeding, bathing, comforting, and loving my daughter with whatever strength I had left. She was my anchor, my reason, my reminder that everything I was doing had a purpose.I didn't complain.I didn't stop.I didn't allow myself to break.

Because every time I looked at her, I saw the life I wanted to give her — a life far from the one I grew up in. A life where she didn't have to worry about money, or shame, or survival. A life where she could dream freely.My responsibilities grew even bigger when my family started leaning on me.Bills.Food.Emergencies.Unexpected needs.

I became the person they called — even when they once doubted me, judged me, and spoke harsh words that left scars I still carry.But I helped anyway.Not because I forgot what they said, but because I knew what it felt like to have nothing.And I refused to let my daughter or my family feel that kind of emptiness again.

During those years, I also worked as a volunteer census surveyor for the Philippine Statistics Authority — a two-month job that tested every ounce of strength I had. It was risky and exhausting, but I accepted it without hesitation. I had to survey the entire town, making sure no household was skipped. Some homes were deep in the fields, others across streams of river that I had to cross, rain or shine. I walked under the heat, under the rain, through mud, through slippery rocks — all for the sake of earning. While other trainees talked excitedly about what they would buy with their salary, I was excited for something else: to finally treat my small family to good food, to sit in a restaurant for the first time, to give them a moment of comfort. And it happened. That simple meal felt like a celebration of every sacrifice I had made.

There were days when I felt like I was carrying the weight of the world — working, selling, mothering, helping, surviving. But there was also a strange strength in it. A strength that came from knowing I was building something real. Something solid. Something mine.

This was the beginning of my multitasking life — the life of a young mother, a provider, a daughter, a sister, a worker, a dreamer. The life of a woman who refused to let her past define her future. And even though it was exhausting, overwhelming, and sometimes lonely, it was also empowering. Because for the first time, I wasn't just surviving anymore.

CHAPTER 19
BECOMING THE FAMILY'S BREADWINNER

When I started working, I thought I was only working for myself and my daughter. I didn't realise that life was slowly shaping me into something bigger — the person my family would eventually depend on. The girl they once doubted, judged, and underestimated was becoming the woman who would carry them through their own storms. It didn't happen overnight.

It happened in small moments — moments of choosing responsibility over rest, courage over fear, and love over resentment.

My job at the travel agency became my first stable source of income, but it wasn't enough. I still sold items on the side, still grabbed every opportunity that came my way, still pushed myself beyond exhaustion because I knew I couldn't afford to stop. Every peso mattered. Every sale mattered. Every hour mattered.

But before I even landed that job, I went through a long season of rejection. After graduation, I applied to so many companies — offices, banks, private businesses — but nothing came. Not a single call back. I even tried working as an accountant in an appliance center, but the management was harsh. They deducted mistakes from our already small salary. As a newbie, I made errors — typing checks on a typewriter, missing a few cents in the accounting, losing receipts I didn't realise were misplaced. I was learning, but they didn't care. So I left.

I had no choice but to tap people in the government — the mayor's office, the governor's office — asking if there were any vacancies. I walked from one office to another, carrying my documents, my courage, and my hope. I didn't care if people judged me for asking. I needed a job. I needed to provide.

And finally, after one interview, I landed a position in the hospital — not as a nurse, but as a health insurance analyzer and encoder. It wasn't the job I once dreamed of, but it was honest work. It was stable. It was something I could build on. I left the travel agency and embraced this new chapter, grateful for the genuine people I met — people with dreams for their families, people who accepted me for who I was, not for who I used to be.

I worked from morning until afternoon, and I left Hanie with my mother. She wanted to take care of her, and I appreciated that. I made sure to contribute to the house — food, money, whatever was needed. It felt good to help my mother, to rebuild something between us, to start a healthier relationship after everything we had been through.

As my responsibilities grew, my family began to lean on me more.Bills.Food.Emergencies.Unexpected needs.I became the person they called, even when they once believed I would never amount to anything.

But I didn't complain.I didn't remind them of the words they once threw at me.I didn't say, "You didn't believe in me before."Because deep inside, I knew what it felt like to have nothing.And I refused to let my family feel that kind of emptiness again.

Being the breadwinner wasn't just about money.It was about emotional strength — the kind that doesn't break even when you're tired, even when you're hurting, even when you feel unseen. It was about waking up every day knowing people depended on you, and still choosing to show up.

There were days when I felt like I was carrying the weight of the world — working, selling, mothering, helping, surviving. Days when I wanted to rest but couldn't. Days when I cried quietly at night because the pressure felt too heavy. But every time I looked at my daughter, I remembered why I was doing all of it.

She was my purpose.My anchor.My reminder that I had to keep going.And as I continued working different jobs, juggling responsibilities, and supporting my family, something unexpected happened — people began to see me differently. The same town that once whispered about me now looked at me with respect. The same relatives who once judged me now asked for advice. The same people who once doubted me now admired my strength.

I didn't become the breadwinner because I wanted to prove anything.I became the breadwinner because life demanded it — and I answered.This chapter of my life wasn't glamorous. It wasn't easy. It wasn't filled with applause or recognition. It was filled with long nights, early mornings, sacrifices, and silent victories. But it was also the chapter that shaped me into the woman I am today — strong, capable, resilient, and unafraid of responsibility.I didn't just provide for my family.I carried them.And in doing so, I discovered a strength I never knew I had.

CHAPTER 20
THE WEIGHT OF EXPECTATIONS AND WHEN SACRIFICE BECOMES A WAY OF LIFE

By the time I settled into my job at the hospital, I thought I finally had a stable path. I wasn't a nurse, but I worked as a health insurance analyzer and encoder — a job that taught me discipline, accuracy, and patience. I was earning enough to survive, enough to help my family, enough to raise my daughter. But "enough" is never enough when you are the breadwinner. Life always asks for more.

One afternoon, my boss called me into her office. She spoke gently, almost carefully, as if she knew her words would change something in me. She told me she had learned that I passed the Licensure Examination for Teachers — an achievement I had buried, forgotten, never used. She said she believed I had more opportunities waiting for me in teaching, especially with the K to 12 program launching in 2016. By January, the Department of Education would be hiring across the region.

She looked at me and said, "Zandy, go for the interview. If you pass, take it. If not, stay here. Either way, you will not lose anything."

I didn't feel excited. I didn't feel nervous. I didn't feel anything.I just said, "Okay, I'll try," without much thought. Teaching wasn't my focus. My mind was too full of responsibilities to dream.On my way home, I told my father about the opportunity. He didn't hesitate. "Go for it," he said. "So you can make more money and help us more. The hospital doesn't pay much." I expected that. For him, everything was always about money. But before I walked away, he added something that pierced me deeper than he realised:

"At least you can pay what you've brought to us in this family."

I froze. After all the years of working, sacrificing, carrying responsibilities that weren't mine alone... To him, I still hadn't "paid" enough. A part of me felt anger — not loud, but quiet, heavy, painful.

When I told my mother I wouldn't be going to work the next morning because I wanted to try applying for the teaching job, she said, "Okay, but make sure you pass. For sure you won't be a teacher. Just stay where you are. You're earning already." For them, my salary wasn't enough.

For me, it wasn't enough either — not for the life I wanted to build, not for the dreams I carried, not for the responsibilities on my shoulders. Working as a government staff was stable, but stability doesn't feed dreams. Stability doesn't lift families out of poverty. Stability doesn't change destinies.

So I didn't listen. I went to the interview. And I failed. I went back to my boss and told her what happened. She didn't scold me. She didn't pity me. She simply said, "That's only one. There will be more, Zandy. A lot of rejections will come. Try again."

Her words lit something inside me — a spark I didn't know I still had.The following week, I tried again.This time, I focused.This time, I believed.This time, I carried not just my dreams, but the weight of every expectation placed on me.And I passed.Everything happened so fast.I was accepted that same day.

And the next morning, I had to report to my new job.It felt unreal — like life had opened a door I didn't even knock on properly. But that's how sacrifice works. When you give everything, even when no one sees it, life eventually gives something back.

This chapter of my life taught me that expectations will always be heavy — from family, from society, from the people who think they know what you owe them. But sacrifice becomes a way of life when you choose to rise anyway. When you choose to keep going even when the world doubts you. When you choose to believe in yourself even when no one else does.And in that moment, stepping into my new job, I realised something important:I wasn't just carrying expectations anymore.I was carrying purpose.

CHAPTER 21
THE REMOTE CLASSROOM AND THE DISTANCE IN MY HEART

Becoming a teacher in a remote area was another chapter I never expected, but life has a way of placing you exactly where you need to be. The school was far from where I lived — long rides, dusty roads, and quiet mornings where the mountains felt like the only witnesses to my new beginning. But I said yes. I said yes for my family, for my daughter, and for the future I was still trying to build.

Teaching in that place taught me patience all over again.Endurance all over again.Humility all over again.It was a new environment, a new community, a new set of challenges. The students came from different backgrounds, each with their own stories, struggles, and personalities. Some were kind, some were difficult, some were lost, and some reminded me of the child I once was — trying to survive quietly.

As the years passed, I learned that being a teacher wasn't just about lessons and grades. It was about understanding people. It was about carrying their stories without letting them break you. It was about giving pieces of yourself even when you were tired.But even in that new world, I couldn't escape judgment.Whenever I openly shared parts of my life — my struggles, my past, my journey — I realised not everyone would understand. Not everyone would care. Some listened with empathy, but many listened only to judge. That was the moment I learned that vulnerability is a gift, but not everyone deserves to hold it.Still, I kept helping my family.Still, I kept providing.Still, I kept lifting our livelihood little by little.Everyone relied on me — except my father.

Two years into teaching, I came home one weekend like I always did. My mother was crying. I asked her what happened, and she finally told me the truth:My father was into drugs again.He was on the list.He was hiding somewhere.
I calmed her down, even though inside me, something felt like it was breaking again. I tried to think of solutions, and eventually, we managed to resolve the situation. But deep inside, I wasn't surprised. I had known for years. I caught him once when I was in high school. I saw it with my own eyes. And from that moment, something inside me changed.

I was angry.Not just at what he did, but at what it meant for us — for our family, for our future, for the responsibilities that fell on me because he chose a different path.When he left for months, I became in charge of everything.I built our house — the house they lived in.Four rooms.A big kitchen.Concrete walls.Tiled floor.Furniture bought from every peso I earned. We had a bathroom now.It was comfortable.It was safe.It was home.

But when my father came back, he returned to a life I had built — not him. And my mother never thanked me. For her, it was simply repayment for the shame I brought, for the sacrifices she made. It wasn't new to me. I had lived with that kind of thinking all my life. And honestly, it was fine. As long as my daughter had a comfortable life, I could carry the rest.

But something changed between me and my father.Our relationship grew distant.Maybe it was the childhood wounds.Maybe it was the disappointments.Maybe it was the years of silence between us.I didn't talk to him much.I didn't look at him much.He was angry with me too — angry at anyone who tried to correct him, advise him, or remind him of what he needed to stop doing. He didn't care. Or maybe he didn't know how to show that he cared.

But sometimes, I saw him alone outside the house, watching the sunset, a cigarette in his hand, his face heavy with thoughts he never said out loud. In those moments, I knew he wanted to say sorry. I knew he wanted to talk gently, to be the father he once was. But he didn't know how. He didn't know where to start. And I didn't know how to reach him either.So we stayed in that distance — two people connected by blood, separated by years of pain, regret, and unspoken words.

And yet, even with all of that, I kept going.For my daughter.For my family.For the life I was building with my own hands. Teaching in that remote area didn't just teach me patience.It taught me how to carry love and disappointment at the same time.It taught me how to show up even when my heart was tired.It taught me that sometimes, the hardest distances are not measured in kilometers, but in memories.

CHAPTER 22
THE TURNING POINT

When my father came home again, nothing had changed — except that everything had gotten worse. He was drunk almost every night, wild toward anyone who crossed his path, careless with his words, and still trapped in the same darkness he had been fighting for years. The drugs were still there. The anger was still there. The distance between us was still there.

And in the middle of all that chaos, life surprised me again. I became pregnant. On January 15, 2020, I gave birth to my baby boy — my lockdown baby, Zach. The world was shutting down, and so was my freedom to move. I was stuck at home for almost a year, unable to travel back to my teaching job. I took a leave, not because I wanted to, but because I had no choice. The world was changing, and so was my life.

During that time, my father was strangely gentle. Maybe it was fear of the virus. Maybe it was the fact that he couldn't go anywhere. Maybe it was because I was home, and he knew we weren't talking much. But he softened. He stayed quiet. He stayed calm. And as Zach grew, my father grew attached to him — and even more attached to my eldest. He loved his grandkids deeply, in a way he didn't always know how to show with his own children.

As months passed, I opened a few small businesses. Slowly, I started succeeding. People in town noticed the changes in my life — the improvements, the growth, the stability I was building with my own hands. And my father noticed too. I could feel it. Even without words, I knew he was proud. We started talking a little more, and the conversations felt lighter, safer, more human.

But while one part of my life was rising, another part was falling apart.My marriage was failing.I was fighting for it, trying to hold on, trying to balance everything — motherhood, work, responsibilities, expectations — but I was exhausted. I didn't know how to carry it anymore. The pain was too much. The effort felt endless. I was breaking quietly, the way women often do when they're trying to be strong for everyone else.

My father saw it.He felt it.And one day, he spoke to me gently — something he rarely did. He told me that whatever I decided, he would support me.Those words touched me deeply.For the first time in a long time, I felt seen by him.Even my mother supported me. She knew how tired I was, how much I had endured, how much I had tried. I was ready to give up on my marriage because I couldn't carry the pain anymore. It was too heavy, too draining, too much for one heart to hold.

But beneath my father's sudden softness, I sensed something else.Something heavier.Something he wasn't saying.He was sick.I didn't know the full truth yet, but I could feel it — in the way he moved, in the way he looked at us, in the way he tried to be present even when he didn't know how. It was as if he was trying to fix small pieces of himself before time ran out.

This was the turning point — not just in my marriage, not just in my career, but in my understanding of life itself.

Everything was shifting. Everything was changing. And I was standing in the middle of it all, holding my children, my responsibilities, my heartbreak, and the quiet fear of losing the father I had spent my whole life trying to understand.

CHAPTER 23
WHEN EVERYTHING FELL ON MY SHOULDERS

There are seasons in life when the weight becomes too much, when every part of your world seems to crumble at the same time. This was that season for me. I felt pressure from every direction — my failing marriage, my own emotions, my children who needed me, and the businesses I had worked so hard to build slowly collapsing under the weight of everything else.

And then there was my father. He was in and out of the hospital, each time with a new diagnosis, a new complication, a new fear. Kidney stones. Diabetes. High blood pressure. Prostate cancer. Lung infection. Cholecystitis. It felt like every part of his body was failing, and with it, every part of my life was becoming more complicated. I was drowning in responsibilities I never asked for, but couldn't walk away from.

I had to borrow money again — from anyone who would listen, anyone who would help. I tapped people I barely knew, swallowed my pride, and begged for loans just to keep him alive. Every hospital bill felt like a mountain. Every prescription felt like another reminder that I was carrying too much. And on top of that, I still had to sustain my children, my mother, and my brother. I was the only one working. The only one earning. The only one holding everything together.
But the hardest part wasn't the money.
It was the loneliness. No one wanted to hear me. No one wanted to understand. No one believed how much I was

struggling — financially, mentally, emotionally. I was surrounded by people, yet I felt completely alone. I cried quietly, worked silently, and carried everything without a single shoulder to lean on.

My marriage was falling apart, and I didn't have the strength to fix it. My businesses were collapsing, and I didn't have the time to save them. My father was dying slowly, and I didn't have the heart to accept it. My children needed me, and I didn't know how to give them the best version of myself when I was breaking inside.Every day felt like a battle I had to fight alone.

Every night felt like a weight pressing on my chest.Every moment felt like I was running out of strength.But even in that darkness, I kept going.Not because I was strong — but because I had no choice.Because people depended on me.Because life didn't pause just because I was tired.

This was the chapter where I learned what true heaviness felt like.Where I learned that being the strong one is often the loneliest role of all.Where I learned that sometimes, the world doesn't see your pain until you break.But I didn't break.I bent.I cried.I struggled.But I didn't break.And that, in itself, was a quiet kind of victory.

CHAPTER 24
LOSING MY FATHER

There are losses that happen in a moment, and there are losses that happen slowly — quietly — long before the final breath. Losing my father was both.

His body had been failing for years, but I didn't realise how close we were to the end until everything in my life began collapsing at the same time. My marriage was breaking. My businesses were falling apart. My finances were drowning under the weight of loans I took just to keep him alive. And emotionally, I was exhausted — stretched thin between being a mother, a daughter, a provider, and a woman trying to hold herself together.

My father was in and out of the hospital, each time with a new diagnosis that felt heavier than the last. Kidney stones. Diabetes. High blood pressure. Prostate cancer. Lung infection. Cholecystitis. It felt like his body was giving up piece by piece, and I was trying to save him with money I didn't have and strength I didn't know how to find anymore.

I borrowed from anyone who would listen. I tapped people again and again. I swallowed my pride until there was nothing left to swallow. All to keep him alive. All while trying to sustain my children, my mother, and my brother. All while feeling completely alone. No one wanted to hear me. No one wanted to understand. No one believed how heavy everything was

— financially, mentally, emotionally.I carried the weight of an entire family on my shoulders, and yet I felt invisible.And then, slowly, my father began to fade.

He wasn't the loud, wild, unpredictable man he used to be.He wasn't the angry man who pushed people away.He wasn't the father who didn't know how to say sorry.

He became quiet.Soft.Gentle in a way I hadn't seen since I was a child.Sometimes I would catch him staring at me — not with anger, but with something like regret. Something like love. Something like a man who wanted to fix things but didn't know how.He watched my children with tenderness.He watched me with pride he didn't know how to express.He watched life slipping away from him, and I think he knew it.

The day he became too weak to stand, something inside me broke.Not because I wasn't prepared — but because no one is ever prepared to lose a parent, even a complicated one. I sat beside him, holding a hand that once terrified me, once disappointed me, once shaped me.

A hand that never learned how to hold mine properly, yet somehow still mattered.His breathing grew shallow.His eyes grew distant.His voice faded into whispers I could barely hear.And then, quietly, without drama, without warning, without the chance to say everything we never said — he was gone.

Just like that.A life full of noise ended in silence.I

didn't scream.I didn't collapse.I didn't break the way people expect daughters to break.I just sat there, feeling everything and nothing at the same time — grief, anger, love, relief, guilt, sadness, and a strange kind of peace. Losing him felt like losing a part of my childhood, a part of my pain, and a part of myself.But it also felt like the closing of a chapter I had been carrying for too long.I buried him with respect.With love.With forgiveness he never asked for but somehow deserved.

And as I walked away from his grave, I realised something:I had spent my whole life trying to understand him.Trying to fix him.Trying to carry him.But in the end, I had to let him go — not just from this world, but from the weight he left on my heart.Losing my father didn't just break me.It changed me.It softened me.It freed me.And it taught me that even the most complicated love is still love — and losing it still hurts.

CHAPTER 25
THE WOMAN I HAD TO BECOME AFTER LOSS

Losing my father changed something in me. It wasn't just grief — it was a shift, a quiet awakening, a realization that life was no longer waiting for me to catch up. Everything happened so fast. My father was gone. My marriage ended. And suddenly, I was standing alone with every responsibility in my hands.

There was no time to fall apart. No space to collapse. No one to catch me if I did. I had to stand up — not because I was strong, but because I had no other choice. My children needed me. My mother and brother still depended on me. The bills didn't stop. The world didn't pause. Life kept moving, and I had to move with it.

I knew nobody would ever truly understand my role. Nobody saw the weight I carried. Nobody felt the pressure that lived in my chest every day. Nobody knew the sacrifices I made quietly, the tears I wiped alone, the fears I swallowed just to keep going. But I accepted it. I accepted that my path was different. I accepted that I was meant to carry more.

I accepted that I had to become a woman who could survive storms without shelter. After my father's death, something inside me hardened — not in a bitter way, but in a determined way. I told myself that if life was going to keep testing me, then I would keep rising. I would keep fighting. I would keep building the future I dreamed of, even if I had to do it alone.

And so I made one of the biggest decisions of my life. I chose to leave.I chose to start again.I chose to become an OFW — a migrant worker — in Australia.It wasn't an easy choice.It wasn't a glamorous choice.It wasn't a choice made out of excitement.It was a choice made out of survival.Out of love.

Out of the desire to give my children a life far better than the one I had.I knew leaving meant carrying even more responsibilities.I knew it meant being far from my children.
I knew it meant starting from zero in a foreign land.
I knew it meant working harder than ever before.

But I also knew this:If I stayed, nothing would change.If I stayed, I would drown in the same cycle of struggle.If I stayed, my dreams would die quietly inside me.So I gathered every piece of courage I had left.I packed my bags.I kissed my children.I held my mother.

And I stepped into a new life — alone, scared, but determined.Becoming an OFW wasn't just a job.It was a transformation.It was the moment I became the woman my younger self needed.The woman my children deserved.The woman my father, in his quiet moments of regret, hoped I would become.

After loss, I didn't just survive.I rebuilt.I rose.I became.And this was only the beginning of the woman I was meant to be.

CHAPTER 26
THE LONELINESS OF STARTING OVER

Starting over sounds brave when people talk about it from the outside. But when you're the one living it — when you're the one packing your life into a suitcase, leaving your children behind, stepping into a foreign land with no promises — it doesn't feel brave at all.

It feels lonely. When I arrived in Australia, the silence hit me first. No familiar voices. No children running around. No mother calling my name. No noise from the town I grew up in.
Just me — a woman who had lost her father, ended her marriage, and carried the weight of an entire family on her shoulders.

I had dreamed of a better life, but I never imagined the price of it would be this kind of loneliness. Every morning, I woke up in a room that didn't feel like mine. Every night, I lay in a bed that felt too big, too cold, too quiet. I missed the chaos of home — the noise, the laughter, even the arguments.

I missed my children so deeply that sometimes I had to hold my chest just to breathe through the ache. People think working abroad is easy — that money grows faster, that life becomes lighter. But they don't see the sacrifices. They don't see the tears you hide in the bathroom. They don't see the nights you cry silently because you can't hug your children.
They don't see the guilt that eats you alive.

I worked hard — harder than I ever had.New rules.New systems.New expectations.New culture.Everything was unfamiliar, and I had to learn fast because failure wasn't an option.

I wasn't just working for myself.I was working for my children, my mother, my brother — for the life I promised them.But even with all that purpose, the loneliness stayed.

There were days when I felt invisible.Days when I felt like a stranger in my own skin.Days when I questioned if I made the right choice.Days when I wondered if I was strong enough to survive this new chapter.But slowly, something inside me began to shift.The loneliness didn't disappear — but I learned how to live with it.

I learned how to turn it into discipline.Into focus.Into strength.I reminded myself why I came here.I reminded myself of the life I wanted to build.I reminded myself that starting over is never easy, but it is necessary.

And in the quiet moments — the ones where I felt the most alone — I discovered a version of myself I had never met before:A woman who could survive distance.A woman who could endure silence.A woman who could rebuild her life from the ground up.A woman who could love her children fiercely, even from thousands of miles away. A woman who could stand alone and still rise.Starting over was lonely.But it was also the beginning of my becoming.

CHAPTER 27
LEARNING TO LIVE AGAIN

Starting over in Australia was not the fresh beginning people imagine. It wasn't a clean slate or a peaceful escape. It was a quiet, heavy kind of rebirth — the kind that forces you to face yourself without distractions, without noise, without the familiar chaos of home.

For the first time in my life, I was truly alone. No children running around. No mother calling my name. No responsibilities knocking on my door every second. No father to worry about. No marriage to fight for. Just me — a woman who had survived loss, heartbreak, and years of carrying everyone else. And in that silence, I had to learn how to live again.

And in that silence, I had to learn how to live again. At first, the loneliness felt like a punishment. I missed my children so deeply that the ache became part of my breathing. I missed the noise of home, even the arguments, even the stress. I missed the version of myself who always had someone to take care of. But slowly, the loneliness became something else.

It became space. It became clarity. It became a mirror. I began to see myself not as the girl who was judged, not as the young mother who struggled, not as the daughter who carried her family, not as the wife who tried too hard to save a marriage, not as the woman who lost her father — but as someone new.

Someone who deserved peace.Someone who deserved rest.Someone who deserved to breathe without guilt.Someone who deserved to dream again.Living in Australia taught me things I never learned back home.I learned how to sit with my own thoughts without fear.

I learned how to enjoy silence without feeling empty.I learned how to take care of myself — not because I had to, but because I wanted to.I learned how to build a life that wasn't defined by sacrifice alone.I worked hard, yes — harder than ever.But this time, the work wasn't just for survival.It was for growth.For healing.For becoming.

I discovered new routines, new strengths, new parts of myself I didn't know existed.I learned how to laugh again — not the tired laugh I used to force, but a real one.I learned how to rest without feeling guilty.I learned how to trust myself, to believe that I could build a future that didn't hurt.And slowly, I began to feel something I hadn't felt in years.Hope.

Not the fragile hope that depends on other people.Not the desperate hope that comes from survival.But a quiet, steady hope — the kind that grows from within.

I was learning to live again.Not as the girl shaped by pain.Not as the woman defined by responsibility.But as someone new — someone stronger, softer, wiser.Someone who finally understood that starting over is not the end of a story.It is the beginning of becoming who you were always meant to be

CHAPTER 28
FINDING MYSELF IN A NEW COUNTRY

Australia was never part of my childhood dreams. I didn't grow up imagining myself in a foreign land, far from my children, far from my mother, far from the life that shaped me. But sometimes life pushes you into places you never expected — not to punish you, but to reveal who you truly are.

When I arrived here, I carried nothing but a suitcase, a broken heart, and the weight of every responsibility I had ever held. I wasn't just a migrant. I wasn't just a worker. I wasn't just a mother trying to survive.
I was a breadwinner — the kind whose stories are rarely told.

People see the money sent home, the photos posted online, the "success" of working abroad. But they don't see the loneliness. They don't see the guilt. They don't see the nights spent crying quietly in a room that doesn't feel like home. They don't see the sacrifices that break you and rebuild you at the same time. In Australia, I had to learn how to live again — but I also had to learn who I was without the noise of my past.

For the first time, I wasn't surrounded by judgment. No one knew my history. No one whispered about my mistakes. No one looked at me as the young mother who "ruined her future." No one saw me as the daughter who carried her family's burdens. No one saw me as the woman whose marriage collapsed under the weight of everything she endured.

Here, I was just... me.And that was terrifying.But it was also freeing.I learned how to walk streets where no one knew my name.I learned how to work without feeling watched.I learned how to breathe without guilt.I learned how to rest without feeling lazy.

I learned how to dream without fear.Slowly, I began to find pieces of myself I had lost along the way — the girl who once wanted to study, the woman who wanted to build something of her own, the mother who wanted to give her children a life she never had.I found strength in the silence.I found courage in the distance.I found clarity in the loneliness.

And in those quiet moments, I finally understood something:Being a breadwinner is not just about providing.It is about becoming.It is about becoming the person your family leans on.Becoming the woman who rises even when she is tired.Becoming the mother who sacrifices without applause.Becoming the daughter who carries burdens she never chose.Becoming the survivor who keeps going even when life feels impossible.

Australia didn't just give me a new life.It gave me a new version of myself — one who is stronger, wiser, softer, and braver than the girl who left home.And as I continue to build my life here, I carry with me every chapter of my story — the pain, the sacrifices, the victories, the losses, the love, the responsibilities, the dreams.These are the parts of my life that people don't see.These are the truths behind every smile.These are the sacrifices behind every achievement.These are the moments that shaped me.These are the untold stories of a breadwinner —and they are mine.

CHAPTER 29
THE LIFE I'M BUILDING NOW

My life in Australia is still young, still unfolding, still finding its shape. I am not fully settled, not fully healed, not fully where I want to be — but for the first time in my life, I am building something that belongs to me.

This chapter of my life is quieter than the ones before it. No chaos. No shouting. No constant emergencies. No one knocking on my door asking for help every hour. Just me — learning how to stand on my own feet in a new country, learning how to breathe without fear, learning how to build a life that isn't defined by survival alone.

But even here, even now, one truth has become clearer than ever: As a breadwinner, you can only rely on yourself. It's not bitterness. It's not anger. It's simply reality. I learned it through years of carrying responsibilities that weren't mine alone. I learned it through the silence of people who never asked if I was okay. I learned it through the weight of bills, loans, and sacrifices that only I could solve. I learned it through the loneliness of starting over in a foreign land.

Here in Australia, I am still the provider for my family in the Philippines. I am still the mother who works for her children's future. I am still the daughter who sends support home. I am still the sister who helps when needed. But I am also something more now.

I am a woman who knows her worth. I am a woman who knows her strength. I am a woman who knows that relying on herself is not a burden — it is a power. The life I'm building now is not perfect, but it is honest.

It is steady. It is mine. I wake up each day with purpose — not the desperate kind that comes from survival, but the grounded kind that comes from growth. I work hard, but I also allow myself to rest. I support my family, but I also protect my peace. I love my children fiercely, even from a distance, and I am building a future where they will one day understand why I had to leave.

Australia has taught me that starting over is not about forgetting where you came from. It's about choosing who you want to become. And I am becoming a woman who:
- no longer apologizes for her strength
- no longer hides her pain
- no longer waits for someone to save her
- no longer fears being alone
- no longer doubts her ability to rise

I am building a life with stability, dignity, and hope — a life where my children will grow up knowing that their mother didn't just survive... she transformed. This is the life I'm building now: A life shaped by courage. A life strengthened by loss. A life guided by purpose. A life that finally belongs to me. And as I continue this journey, I carry with me every chapter of my past — not as a weight, but as proof of who I had to become and a woman I become to them.

CHAPTER 30
MY FINAL WORDS

If there is one thing my life has taught me, it is this: Strength is not loud. Strength is not perfect. Strength is not the absence of fear or pain. Strength is choosing to rise again, even when everything inside you wants to give up.

I look back at the girl I once was — the young mother judged by her own community, the daughter who carried responsibilities far beyond her age, the woman who fought for her family even when they didn't always fight for her. I look back at the heartbreaks, the losses, the sacrifices, the nights I cried quietly so no one would hear. I look back at the moments I thought would break me.

And I realise now... they didn't break me. They built me. Every struggle shaped me. Every disappointment taught me. Every sacrifice strengthened me. Every loss opened a new path. Every chapter — even the painful ones — led me here. To this woman. To this life. To this beginning. I am still a breadwinner. I am still a mother. I am still a daughter. I am still a provider. But I am also more than that now.

I am a woman who learned to stand alone. A woman who learned to rebuild her life in a foreign land. A woman who learned to love herself after years of forgetting how. A woman who learned that relying on herself is not loneliness — it is power.

A woman who learned that her story, no matter how heavy, is worth telling.My journey is far from over.Australia is still new.My dreams are still growing.My heart is still healing.My life is still unfolding.But for the first time, I am not afraid of what comes next.

Because I know now that I can survive anything.I know now that I can rise from anything.I know now that I can build a life from nothing.I know now that I can carry the weight of a family and still find myself in the process.These are my final words for this book, but not for my life:

To every breadwinner who feels alone — you are stronger than you think.To every mother who sacrifices quietly — your love is seen.To every daughter who carries burdens she never chose — your courage matters.To every woman who has been judged, doubted, or underestimated — your story is not over.

And to myself —the girl who survived,the woman who rose,the mother who keeps going,the breadwinner who never gave up:You did it.You made it this far.And you will go even farther.This is not the end.This is the beginning of the life you were meant to live.

EPILOGUE

There are stories we live, and there are stories we survive. Mine was both. I began this journey as a young girl who carried too much, too soon.

I walked through judgment, heartbreak, poverty, motherhood, loss, and the weight of being the family's backbone. I became a breadwinner not because I wanted to, but because life demanded it. And in every chapter, I learned that strength is not something you are born with — it is something you build, piece by piece, through every battle you never expected to fight. Today, I stand in a new country, building a new life, still carrying the people I love, but finally learning to carry myself too.

My story is not perfect, but it is real. It is messy. It is painful. It is brave. And it is mine. If there is one truth I want to leave with you, it is this:

You can rise from anything.
You can rebuild from nothing.
You can become someone you never imagined — even after everything you've lost.
These are the untold stories of a breadwinner.
And they continue, every day, with every step I take toward the life I am still creating.

The Untold Stories of a Breadwinner
A memoir of survival, sacrifice, and becoming.

From a childhood shaped by poverty and responsibility, to young motherhood marked by judgment and struggle, to the heartbreak of losing her father and the courage of starting over in a foreign land — Zandra's story is a powerful testament to resilience.

This memoir reveals the hidden battles of a breadwinner: the silent sacrifices, the emotional weight, the loneliness of carrying a family, and the strength it takes to rebuild a life from the ground up.

Raw, honest, and deeply human, The Untold Stories of a Breadwinner is not just a story of hardship — it is a story of transformation.

A story of a woman who refused to break.
A story of a mother who rose again and again.
A story of finding hope, healing, and purpose in the most unexpected places. For anyone who has ever carried more than they could hold —this book is for you.

www.ingramcontent.com/pod-product-compliance
Lightning Source LLC
Chambersburg PA
CBHW041216070526
44583CB00001B/3